DROWNING

GROWING UP IN THE THIRD REICH

GERHARD DURLACHER

Translated by Susan Massotty

First published as *Drenkeling* in 1987 by
Meulenhoff Nederland bv, Amsterdam

This edition first published 1993 by
Serpent't Tail, 4 Blackstock Mews, London N4
and 401 West Broadway #1, New York, NY 10012

A CIP catalogue record for this book is obtainable from the British Library on request

Typeset in 10½/14pt Garamond by Contour Typesetters, Southall, London
Printed in Great Britain by Cox & Wyman Limited,
of Reading, Berkshire

The translator would like to thank Karen Steenhard, Alan Broad and Dr. A. van der Heide for their invaluable assistance.

CONTENTS

DROWNING

PETER'S TRIP TO THE MOON

The fitting room in Kindler's knitwear store smells of old rubber dress shields and the warm familiar mustiness of Grandmother's room. The pins on the parquet floor prick my heel as I hop on one foot and try to aim the other through the leg of a navy-blue sailor suit.

The owner watches my awkward movements with his piercing eyes narrowed into slits, his mean,. mocking mouth compressed into a thin line. My mother, looking beautiful and elegant in her tan foalskin coat, is standing half behind him in quiet shyness and approval. He's an enemy but sells to Jews, I've heard them say at home. The trousers feel uncomfortably long and scratchy above my knees, and it suddenly occurs to me that the nettle shirts Eliza wove for the swan princes in the Andersen fairy tale must have felt like this.

My mirror image returns my angry stare, for the sailor's cap which would have made amends for many things is not to be mine. Instead, I get a cloth cap made of wool that can also serve as the prescribed headgear on holy days. I would prefer a thousand times over to have Lederhosen with nice bone buttons like the boys in the neighborhood wear, but this thought cannot even be uttered aloud.

I feel miserable and angry as the hem of my new breeches chafes against the inside of my ice-cold thighs.

My discomfort is quickly forgotten at the prospect of going with my parents in a few days to see the Christmas performance of *Peter's Trip to the Moon* in the big theater.

In a mist of tiny snowflakes, with the street lights shining like full moons, the three of us walk past the windows of stores and houses. The lighted Christmas trees and Advent wreaths that we don't have at home can be seen through the half-open curtains. Though my mother sympathizes with my longing, Father gruffly brushes aside my wish for a fir tree; after all, we have Hanukkah.

He walks a few steps ahead of us, a giant in a heavy dark coat and stiff black hat with a round brim, the Eden hat. His walking stick, a marvel with a hidden umbrella, is taller than I am. He hardly ever leans on it when walking; instead, he uses it like an extended index finger to point out people and things, and waves it in the air to greet passers-by.

At the corner of Leopold Square, we're joined by a smiling Uncle Rudi, a childhood friend of Father's. He laughs a lot and can sometimes get the deep lines above Father's mouth to soften. From where we're standing, I can see the lighted window of his store, with its display of toys, kitchenware and china. I cherish the cap gun he recently gave me, but unfortunately my supply of caps is gone and may not be replenished.

We walk in the direction of the Spa, which I vaguely

recognize in the misty light from our Sunday morning walks to the Pump Room, a place where old people sip smelly water. We pass grisly murals of armored knights, dragons, snorting horses and terrified maidens which make my skin crawl.

To the left of the Spa, the street lights outside the theater shine through the bare trees on Lichtentaler Allee like a cluster of milky-white balloons. During the walks I took in the summer and fall with my mother and Senta, my black German shepherd, it had never dawned on me that the pink theater building could be transformed into a storybook castle at night.

Uncle Rudi suddenly quickens his pace, runs ahead of us with his trouser legs flapping and points to two oversized snowmen glowing rosily in the reflection from the theater. A thin man, a fat woman and in between them a tall but slender borzoi with eyes made out of coal.

Because of the dog, I recognize the figures: my aunt and her fiancé, an actor with a monocle, a fur collar and pointed shoes. The drivers of the carriages that bring them to the theater every evening had gotten together and immortalized them in snow. Either because they liked them or, as my father observed, because of the handsome tips.

The pink and cream theater façade, the lamp-studded balcony, the chiseled figures under the eaves: everything seems bigger, more beautiful, more impressive than during the daytime. Light twinkles from the numerous arched windows. The middle of the three entrance doors is open wide, and a red carpet greets us at the foot of the stone steps.

Everything around me is a fairy tale. The endless rows of maroon seats, the gently sloping floor, the powder-blue ceiling dotted with rosy cherubs, the various-sized gilt candelabra on the walls, the theatrical masks and round-cheeked trumpeters, the balcony tiers arranged in over-grown fairy rings, the gleaming-red, wavy curtain: every-thing looks like the palace of the king into which I, the tiny Mook, have flown on my magic slippers.

Not too far from the curtain, I shuffle between my parents to the middle of a row of seats and nearly sink through the red plush. Two girls with blonde braids and bows are giggling in back of me. I don't dare turn around.

As the lights slowly dim, the noise dies down under the "shhh" of parents. An air of silent expectation hovers over the theater until the curtain opens on the right to reveal a sleigh with bells and fake white reindeer gliding on to the stage. A small stooped man with a long beard, wearing a fur hat and a brown robe, steps out of the sleigh. On his back is a bulging burlap bag, which he sets down in the middle of the stage with a growl. An excited whisper runs through the rows: "Santa Claus, look, it's Santa Claus." Instead of the fairy tale figure I was hoping for, whose story my parents had read to me at home and whose melodies I knew as bedtime songs, I see Santa Claus with a birch rod in one hand and a sack to carry off naughty children in the other, and the sight terrifies me.

He talks to us from his high and brightly lit spot, but the words go right past me. Then he calls out a name or beckons a child to come to him. The youngsters climb on stage, some of them in tears and others displaying great courage. In a deep voice, he asks whether the child has been bad this year. He puts down his birch and after the boy or girl has sung him a song or recited a poem, he reaches into his bag and pulls out gingerbread and marzipan.

My heart nearly stops beating when I hear my name called. With my face glowing and my eyes filled with tears, I try in vain to get myself off the hook. The temptation of the gingerbread and my mother's reassuring words do nothing to dispel the sinking feeling in my stomach. Then behind me I hear a giggling whisper and the words "scaredy pants" and I furiously push past all the knees on my way to the aisle.

The steps to the stage are higher than I expected, and when I peer into the ravine of the orchestra pit, I forget my fear of Santa Claus. He seems even taller up close. He motions me over amicably and I reluctantly cross the wooden floor until I'm standing beside him. I don't dare look at his face. The birch and the bag hold me in their thrall, and I answer his gruff query about my behavior and my transgressions in a hoarse whisper.

Surely I can't tell him about my misdeeds in Café Schweinfurt where, in my boredom and anger at the lengthy conversation between my aunt and the proprietress, I had stuffed all the chocolate flakes and cherries from a huge white Black Forest cake into my mouth?

Would I like to sing him a song? Or recite a poem? My throat seems to be sealed shut, my head a merry-go-round. He hums the opening bars of a well-known song about a little bird. I try to sing, but no sound seems to come from my mouth. There is a rustle of voices from the audience. He leans forward and offers me his ear to whisper into.

I recognize that ear and then the hair around it, and when I look at his eyes up close, I know that everything is all right. My fear melts away; I could hug him. My throat opens up and I shout with joy: "You're not Santa Claus, you're Uncle Herbert."

I see him start and then stifle a laugh with his lips pressed together when hisses and rippling laughter reach us from below. Why our upstairs neighbor, an actor who frequently drops by for coffee, is suddenly pretending to be Santa Claus is something I don't understand. I sing the song he hummed to me, close by his ear, and am given a large heart-shaped gingerbread cookie. Satisfied and happy, I walk in the glare of the spotlight to the steps alongside the awesome orchestra pit.

As I return to the row where my parents are sitting, people look at me with expressions of laughter or anger on their faces.

I shuffle past the numerous knees to my place. I'm still so wrapped up in my adventure that I don't hear the comments from the audience. The blonde girls in the row behind me pointedly turn their heads away. Their father, his hair cropped close, leans forward and snarls spitefully at me: "Smart-aleck little Jewboy, I'll . . ."

The remainder of his sentence is drowned out by the opening bars of the overture, and with my heart in my mouth, I wait for the curtain to open.

TAPERS AND TORCHLIGHTS

"Boruch"... "Boruch"... "Atto"... "Atto"... "Adonai"... "Adonai": word for word I parrot the incomprehensible blessings after hesitantly attempting to light my candle with another burning, dripping candle. Confused by the solemnity of the moment, I nearly knock over my solitary taper, stuck on to the semi-circular lid of a white cookie tin painted with red roses.

At my side are three stately figures in dark suits and black hats. Their solemn Sabbath faces are lighted by the flickering glow of the three Hanukkah candelabra on the sideboard. My father, Uncle Jacob (Grandmother's younger brother) and "Uncle" Albert, who works for Father but whose relation to the family isn't clear to me even though his last name is the same as ours, lit the first tapers on their menorahs while singing the three blessings in a strange melodic monotone, with Uncle Jacob, as the oldest, going first. I feel ashamed of my ignorance, but also furious because, as the youngest, I'm only allowed to burn a light on that wax-studded lid.

Standing behind me are my grandmother, mother and

aunt, also dressed in their best and wearing shawls over their heads as if it's cold inside. They utter murmurs of approval and sighs of relief when my candle catches flame. I'm finally through repeating all those strange sounds. My grandmother lays her hands on my cap, mutters some Hebrew words and ends with the same word with which I've learned to close my bedtime prayer: omeyn. Then she says in an audible whisper: "When you can recite the broches, the blessings, I'll give you a menorah of your very own."

The package-laden table draws my attention like a magnet away from the Hanukkah song everyone is singing in their own tempo, not paying the slightest attention to my father, who is playing the melody on the piano and trying to keep us all in line with his cantor voice.

Relieved, I carry the hats to the hall. The holiday which Mother thinks resembles Christmas can now begin. A tree, its boughs laden with packages, strings of lights, garlands, nuts and heart-shaped gingerbread, like other children have in their homes, seems much more real to me. Still, the big box on the table manages to dispel my secret fantasy. My fingers are stiff with excitement as I yank the fuzzy string off the package.

Several minutes later, I'm scooting on my knees over our big wide-bordered Persian carpet, which has been transformed into a street over which I'm racing my new red fire truck. Hanukkah is fun too!

In Leopold Square, the huge square I'm never allowed to cross without holding someone's hand, there's a giant fir tree decorated with lights, garlands, silver balls and hundreds of stars. Standing before it is a policeman in a green uniform and black helmet that looks like a bulging flowerpot pulled down over a lump on the back of his head. His arms move up and down and bend at the elbows like a jumping jack. The tooting cars stop and make a stink, circle the tree and disappear down the streets radiating from the traffic cop like a star.

Maria holds my cold fist in her secure, warm hand and squeezes it with pleasure as the tree comes in sight. "It's bigger and more beautiful than ever before," she says with her words floating on a balloon of vapor, and sticks both our hands in her scratchy coat pocket as we stand on the rough paving stones before the broad tree trunk.

The cars have stopped driving past the policeman and it looks like he has nothing more to do. All around us are children with their fathers and mothers. The little girl beside me is wearing boy's shoes and has huge darns in her long brown stockings. Her father is standing alongside her shivering in his baggy suit, as he is without an overcoat. I feel embarrassed among so many poor people, but my shame melts into thin air the moment the music begins to play and "Oh Tannenbaum" pours out of everyone's mouth on clouds of condensation. Maria's high clear voice rises above the other voices and I also dare to sing the song I'm forbidden to sing at home by everyone except Maria. She'll never tell our secrets. She'll always be my warm refuge.

One song follows another, but my feet are cold and my attention is flagging. We thread our way through the musty forest of people to the other side of the square. The reproving stares of the thin, ashen faces make me feel ashamed of my impatience.

From the steps leading to the Town Hall, the graystone knight called Bismarck towers high above the street where my grandmother has her furniture store. A spike sticks out of his white winter cap like a lightning rod. Though he appears to be standing guard, I'm relieved when I enter the store's black marble entryway and his stern gaze can no longer follow me.

Maria has to ring the brass doorbell a few times before a light appears behind the shadowy furniture and carpet rolls.

I recognize Aloïs, the man who waxes and polishes, by his skate-like walk and flapping dustcoat. In search of the keyhole, he rattles the doorknob with trembling fingers. Absentminded and friendly, he looks at us with his dark wet eyes and mumbles "Merry Christmas" from under his walrus mustache as if it embarrasses him.

He shuffles ahead of us back toward the light, wafting brandy and methylated spirits in his trail. I recognize the smell. It had recently filled our music room, where Aloïs, moving his arms in smooth circles and puffing like a steam engine, spent nearly two days polishing our Ibach grand piano to a shine. Mother's whispered words about his drinking aroused my sympathy, and I'm glad he's been invited to the forthcoming Christmas party.

The spooky room is filled with soft armchairs and sofas, wooden and brass bedsteads piled with Pullman mattresses, heavy bow-legged tables and towering sideboards. I let go of Maria's hand and seek forbidden adventure on the bouncy box springs.

I hear my name called in full from the lighted doorway. Although the message gets lost in wool, plush and bouclé, I know that my voyage of discovery must end and that the party is about to begin.

The office in the back of the store is bathed in light and looks a lot more cheerful than usual. On weekdays, the old, worn desks and tables are piled with paper, inkstands, blotting paper and merry-go-rounds with rattling rubber stamps, but today they are hidden under Mother's white tablecloths and decorated with red ribbons and fresh fir boughs. Large Christmas wreaths, onto which white candles have been clamped with tin clothespins, are suspended with twine from the smoke-stained ceiling. I know better than to look for a Christmas tree. At home, Grandmother had shrilly drawn the line at the wreaths. As she sees it, a tree is something like ham or bacon.

Underneath the wreaths, the white damask tablecloths represent the land of plenty. The various cakes, cinnamon stars and Christmas candies hold me spellbound. Only after being gently admonished by Mother do I shake hands with the employees I know well along with the ones I'm less familiar with and wish them a Merry Christmas.

They are seated on chairs and crates like guests in their own office, all of them dressed in their Sunday best except for Aloïs, who is still wearing his dustcoat.

My diminutive gray-haired grandmother is enthroned on a new armchair from the showroom. The lace collar on her black dress gleams though the loose-weave shawl draped over her shoulders. Her veined right hand rests on a black cane with a silver knob, and when she says something to my mother or my Dutch aunt about the food or the packages on the table in the shadow beside her chair, she points with the cane to press home her point.

My uncle's wife frowns in annoyance at this gesture from behind her thick, gleaming glasses. When her husband makes a move to start the gift-giving with a speech, she whispers audibly that my father should do this. I feel proud when he unhesitatingly assumes this responsibility and, curious about what's in the packages, I watch how he places a gift, on which a name is written, into the hands of each employee and makes a remark that makes everyone laugh.

Martha, the blonde salesgirl whose hair is braided over her ears like headphones, twists off the cap of a large bottle of 4711 eau de cologne and sprinkles a few drops on my clean handkerchief.

Aloïs hesitates, not knowing whether to open his bottle of cognac, but decides to wait until he's home when Mother promises him schnapps.

Gersbach, Father's chauffeur, who can barely squeeze himself into a car without banging his close-cropped head, laughs in relief as his large hands glide effortlessly into a new pair of yellow gloves. Standing in front of the mirror, he dons his new silk tie and bursts into sudden song. My father joins in, and the *Pearl Fishers' Duet*, which always fills the car during their long trips, startles some and makes others laugh.

Grandmother's brother-in-law, Uncle Adolf, stares straight

ahead, frowning. His wrinkled face looks less wrinkled than usual because of the big bandage on his forehead. An "encounter with the Brownshirts," I hear Grandmother mutter in disapproval, but I don't really know what that means.

No thought had been given to a present for him because he's supposed to celebrate Hanukkah but doesn't. The package meant for Willy, the recently vanished bookkeeper, is given to Uncle Adolf instead. The cigars don't make him any more cheerful.

Gersbach teasingly begins the opening bars of a Christmas carol, but stops before long because only Martha chimes in a few notes.

Maria, my mother and my aunt slice the cakes, pass around the candies and cookies and pour the coffee and schnapps while my grandmother watches as if she's not really aware of what's going on. Her pince-nez falls into her lap.

I hear the buzz of voices coming from far away and see the Christmas party fade slowly through the filmy windows of my sleep.

Maria is reading aloud from the fat book of fairy tales whose scary pictures usually give me a secret thrill, but I'm not really listening tonight. My infinite curiosity is aroused by the snatches of conversation about the Silvester Ball which can be heard through the open bedroom door.

My parents are dressing for the party. This afternoon, after washing my hands, I was allowed to gently touch my father's tall black hat, my mother's long white kid gloves and their black and white silk masks. Later, in a clandestine moment, I had made faces at the mirror, with the black mask which was much too large for me on my nose.

I say goodbye in the hallway. My mother lifts the voile over the brim of her hat. I may only plant a very gentle goodnight kiss on her velvety powdered cheek. Since lipstick smears, her kiss tonight feels like the breeze in the wake of a butterfly. I've never seen my parents look as beautiful as they do this evening, even more beautiful than the pictures in *Illustrierte*.

The clips in the corners of Mother's square-necked black crêpe de Chine gown flash blue and green. The eyes of the fox around her neck peer sleepily from the gray fur, as if it were overwhelmed by her perfume.

My father straightens his white bow tie, after grumblingly re-attaching the stud to the stiff collar of his barn-door shaped white shirt front.

Once Maria closes the front door behind them, quiet again descends on the apartment. Far away, a car roars and bells chime in anticipation of New Year's Day 1933.

A soft tinkle of silverware and plates comes from the dining room. Maria is making breakfast, but she and I are the only ones awake this first Sunday.

The church bells are ringing longer and louder than usual. I flee the feathery warmth of my bed and keep pestering Maria until she finally agrees to take me to her church.

Holding Maria's hand, I walk through the prickly-cold winter air, from which no snow seems to want to fall, to the big yellow church with the tall spires on the square where the doctor also lives. My mother never wants to go inside, but now I finally have a chance to see what's hidden there.

A lot of shivering people are standing bareheaded beside hard wooden pews. The ceiling and chandeliers are eerily high. Organ music rumbles through my stomach like thunder and the minister's throaty warble resounds from every side. I can't understand a word, even though I know it isn't Hebrew. The mystery is disappointing, and on the way home, long before the last hymn, I confess that her church doesn't seem that fun to me.

From behind the front door comes the murmur of visitors. No one asks us where we've been. Friends of my parents are talking excitedly and waving their hands and arms in the air to emphasize their words. Some of them are still wearing their hats just like in the synagogue. The fat cantor with the big shiny nose has turned red. He looks furious. My parents look like they haven't had enough sleep and Father's voice sounds flat.

While Maria helps make coffee, my mother tells her what happened at the New Year's ball. All ears, I catch snatches of a story that resembles a highly sinister fairy tale.

A ball with masks, dances, music and champagne. Men dressed like princes in old uniforms and powdered wigs. Women in white corkscrew curls, lace and wide hoop skirts. Silken facial masks and masks shaped like pigs and cows and lions. Chimney sweeps and Cinderellas, clowns and nymphs, Pierrots and peasants. Colorful confetti everywhere and streamers like giant spiderwebs ensnaring the revelers.

And then the clocks chime the new year, champagne corks pop, Christmas crackers bang and masks are removed.

Only one person, the elegant pasha in a turban and saber, keeps his face hidden. In his white-gloved hands, he holds a beautifully decorated box of rich bonbons. Bowing lithely, he makes the rounds, presenting his sweet offer with a courtly gesture to Jewish ladies and an occasional gentleman. My mother declines, even after his friendly insistence. Champagne and chocolate don't go very well together, she thinks, but many of the others accept readily.

No one knows exactly when he arrived and he disappears just as suddenly.

The party continues on its merry way and then all of a sudden Mrs. Roos feels ill. Gasping for air, both hands clutched to her stomach, she runs to the hall, where the women who have arrived ahead of her are banging in desperation on toilet doors.

There is a wild melee, with weeping women in soiled dresses. My mother tries to help. Like the others who spurned the bonbons, she hasn't been affected.

A group of Jewish men, reinforced by German friends, set out to look for the imposter, but don't find him. Their booty merely consists of the turban and the empty box with the words "Jews Stink, Heil Hitler" written on the bottom in bold black letters. Signed with a swastika.

*

Using one of my mother's five-mark coins, I make portholes in the ice flowers of the January windowpanes and watch the whirling snowflakes. I want to whizz down the slopes tomorrow on my new Davos sled, just like other children, and I wish for a world enveloped in white.

My father emerges from behind the newspaper which makes him invisible every morning and evening. In turn, my grandmother disappears behind the paper screen with her pince-nez on her nose. She quarrels with her brother who now comes to visit her almost daily about who may read the paper first. There's a lot of angry grumbling about Adolf, surely someone other than my elderly uncle with the bandaged head. Father twirls the two knobs on the whining and crackling cabinet radio until he hears voices which are also talking about Adolf, except that the last name doesn't sound the same.

No one is interested in snow, and lying in my bed I dream of how soft and white it is outside.

Though the atmosphere at home is far from cheerful, January does bring outdoor fun. On Sundays, seated behind Father, Mother or Maria, I swoosh down the hill in back of the theater. Or screaming with pleasure and fright, we roll over the bumpy snow when our tiny vehicle decides to make a run for it without us. I watch in envy as the other children race past us in pairs like consummate tobogganists, and keep my mouth shut when they jeer at us after a spill.

The weekdays are boring. Hardly anyone has any time for me. All they do is read the newspaper and listen to the voices coming from the radio. Father complains about business and Mother about the stores where it's almost impossible to buy butter, eggs and meat. Time and again I hear the names of strange men far away in Berlin: Von Papen, Hindenburg or Schleicher and the Hitler who is also called Adolf, just like my uncle.

It gets colder every day.

The ice flowers on the windows are thicker every morning, and the tennis courts on Lichtentaler Allee are filled with skaters wearing knitted caps, knickerbockers and bulky wool sweaters. Father also straps a pair of skates to his climbing boots and glides unsteadily over the ice. Mother and I watch and chuckle. When he falls, she scurries to the fence, but he's already scrambled to his feet. He tries a few more steps and then gives up.

On the way to his brother's house, I look forward to seeing my cousins' rabbits and marmots. The cages have been put in the sun porch because of the cold. Like proud ringmasters, my cousins take the animals through their paces and tell me about the long trip to Holland they're going to make soon.

The house is filled with packing crates, and their toys have been wrapped in newspapers and straw and tucked away where it's impossible to find them. My aunt has traveled on ahead to unfamiliar Rotterdam and they're going to follow soon with my uncle. Their excitement makes me sad, since I don't have very many friends to play with as it is.

Although there are still some skaters on the iced-over

tennis courts the last Sunday in the month, it isn't very crowded. Many of them have pinned to their coats a round red and white pin with a black swastika in the middle. Children walking along holding their mother's hand or standing at the edge of the sidewalk are carrying paper flags with the same symbol.

Far away, drums are banging out the beat of a military march and as the forest of flags, banners and gleaming instruments comes into view, the band begins to play the Horst Wessel song in heavy, ominous tones. Hundreds of jackbooted men in brown shirts, riding breeches, Sam Browne belts and helmets whose straps cut their chins in two march strictly to the beat like marionettes, their eyes boring into the necks of the men in front. Wound around their left arms is a red armband with the black hooked cross on a field of white. The Horst Wessel song pours forth from their throats in a raucous staccato: "Raise high the flags! Stand rank on rank together."

Enormous flags flutter high above their heads and sparks fly from their heels just like the horses from the brewery. The ground trembles under the stomp of boot soles and windowpanes tinkle in the narrow streets.

I pull my mother along, in order to see more, hear more. She doesn't want to stay there among the flag-waving children and their arm-waving parents. I follow her unwillingly to our apartment. We thread our way past stores and houses, behind the backs of the crowd. Between the outstretched arms and flags, I see the tail end of the parade march past to pounding drums. The door to our apartment on the other side of the street seems impossible to reach.

I'm surrounded on all sides by children, older and younger than I am, proudly clutching their flags. I feel naked and excluded as I'm dragged along against my will by my mother and the heavy door shuts behind me.

The marching music fades slowly away. Sitting in Father's chair, my mother throws her hands over her eyes and tears drip on to her winter coat.

My kindergarten is closed the next day. The long steep walk past the Spa and all the stores has been for nothing. The photographer, standing beside her shop door, asks Mother what she thinks of the pictures in the display window. One of them is of me, with chubby cheeks and a sickly sweet smile.

Men are standing in the cold beside the kiosk, reading their newspapers and sending up clouds of cigar smoke. Many more policemen than usual are patrolling the streets today.

At home, today is washday. Maria is standing in the basement in a veil of vapor doing the washing and Mother is feeding sheets through the wringer. Upstairs in the kitchen, cabbage rolls are simmering on the stove. In the stairwell, I smell this typical Monday-is-washday dish, which I absolutely loathe, at the neighbors' as well.

During lunch, everybody keeps quiet and listens to the voices coming from the radio. I don't dare complain about the food for fear of a harsh reprimand from my father. But when I eat slowly and toy with the cabbage on my plate, nobody scolds me.

My mother puts her finger to her lips. All of a sudden the

voices on the air fall silent too. Forks and knives freeze in midair. A hoarse, excited voice reports from Berlin that the new Chancellor of the German Reich is . . . Adolf Hitler. Adolf, just like my uncle.

He's sitting at the table with us today and turns as white as the bandage on his head. My parents also look shocked. Maria brings the half-eaten plates back to the kitchen, but no one is thinking of dessert. I don't understand what it all means, but I feel relieved when Father says that it can't last long and that there's no need to worry.

An air of restlessness prevails in the street below. There are many more Brownshirts and people on the streets today than usual. My grandmother prefers to remain indoors, but my mother can't decide whether or not to go outside.

Military music blares from the radio all afternoon, and men talk about the government and what it will do for the country. On the counter at the bakery is a vase filled with red swastika-emblazoned paper flags. Each of the children ahead of me gets one, or sometimes two. The baker's wife assumes I won't be singing tonight in the square outside the theater and that therefore I don't need a flag. My mother agrees with her wholeheartedly and that makes me really mad. My cousin, who's not much bigger than I am, is allowed to go. Grownups are so unfair, I think, but I keep my mouth shut and don't say it aloud.

The strange day seems to have come to an end after dinner. When the dishes have been done, the plates and platters stacked in the buffet, the silverware put away properly in its tray and everyone has been given a goodnight kiss, Maria tucks me in bed.

In the semi-darkness of my nursery, I lay the ghosts of my childish fears to rest and hug my ragged teddy bear to me. I hear a loud boom, then another one, followed by a heavy drum roll and a rat-a-tat-tat. A tuba groans and trumpets blare.

Wide awake, shocked and excited, I jump out of bed, run to the living room and see my parents and the others standing by the open window. The lamp has been switched off, but the flickering light from below casts their giant shadows on the wall.

Kneeling on a chair, wrapped in Grandmother's shawl, I look outside and see something that makes me speechless. On both sides of the street, as far as the eye can see, there are long rows of torchlights, like curling snakes of fire. The cold, damp air quivers like turbulent water. Under their helmets, the faces of the Brownshirts reflect the flames. Hundreds of devils stamp their hooves on the granite paving stones and roar their song. Flags flutter above the flames and cast black shadows on the houses. Men of iron wearing helmets of steel pound their boots on the anvil of the street.

At the head of the procession is a man astride a horse, with a tiger skin for a saddle. Underneath his helmet, the flames play across his stony face. In front of and to either side of the tiger skin are barrel-sized drums strung with cords and painted with wolf's teeth, like predatory jaws.

He beats the taut skin of each drum in turn with thickly encased drumsticks, taps out a few drumrolls, throws the sticks in the air and catches them again like a juggler. And all that in time to the boots.

Proud, menacing and unassailable, he rides past, the cruel knight in my fairy-tale book.

I follow him with my eyes until he's out of sight and hear my father, reminded of Schubert, whisper softly: "the Erl King."

BIRTHDAY

My aunt, back again from the faraway land of butter, cheese and eggs, is like a guest in her own home.

The greasy, travel-battered package she gives my mother is put in the pantry under lock and key: a precious gem.

"Dutch butter and Dutch cheese," she says, emphasizing the "Dutch," since everything is better there, according to her.

It makes me think of green grass and fat Holstein cows in a mountainless landscape, the horizon nothing more than a stripe; a picture in my aunt's nearly empty house.

For me she has a flat box with fluffy kittens on the lid. A long row of chocolate cat tongues is nestled in a white bed of satin, too beautiful to eat.

The way she says my name is so funny. It's as if she's clearing her throat when she says the G, and sometimes I don't understand what she says. "That's because she's Dutch," Grandmother confided to me with a note of pity in her laugh.

She argues with my parents and wants to talk them into moving to her watery country as well. My father thinks this is a lot of nonsense and panicky behavior. He doesn't want to believe her scare stories.

Her eyes look angry through the thick lenses because my father is deaf to her words, and when she says goodbye, she points to me and says: "Do it for him."

A man is standing at the front door in an overly long, soiled, moth-eaten overcoat with a black velvet collar. A dark, greasy Homburg is perched on his head. White lines are etched above the hatband like faint snow-capped mountains, and his long brown hair curls out from under the brim. The melancholy folds around his eyes and mouth make him look like our dentist's friendly old bloodhound.

He's holding a scratched and battered suitcase in his left hand, with a scruffy violin case tucked under the arm. He's using the other arm to lean against the doorjamb for support. I can only understand from his whining German that he wants to talk to my "mama" or "papa."

Mother comes up the stairs. She isn't really startled to see the man at the front door. I recognize her look of concern and pity, for he isn't the first refugee to knock at our door for food, shelter or money.

Seated in the kitchen beside a plate of sandwiches, he tells his story, between bites. I can only understand snatches of it.

It seems he has to go back to Poland. He isn't allowed to stay in Germany any longer. Hawking wares on the street has been forbidden, and the Brownshirts have beat him with their clubs and fists. They mock his Yiddish German, and even the German Jews are sometimes hard-hearted. He wants to sell us his violin, but Father is suspicious and refuses. He lowers the price, but finally snaps the dingy case shut when Father rather irritably stuffs a few bills in his coat pocket.

That evening, in the warm, steamy bathroom, my mother wraps me in a large white terrycloth towel and suddenly throws her arms around me. Her eyes are wet: "That can't happen to us, it can't be true." And she smiles through her tears and whispers decidedly: "And we're going to celebrate Father's birthday, boycott or no boycott."

The round, white, marble-topped tables, anchored firmly to the ground on iron lion's legs, are practically empty. Only two silver-haired old ladies are sitting beside the window, stirring their coffee. The fat pastry cook, clad in a stiff white apron, slices off two generous portions of Black Forest cake topped with cherries and chocolate flakes, eases them onto some plates and shuffles towards their table with the plates in her hands.

On her way back to my mother, in the back of the café, she gives me a friendly nod, making her rosy cheeks and chubby double chins wobble. She points to the pretzels on the counter and allows me to take a few.

My gaze is riveted on the contents of the display case: half and whole cakes decorated with chocolate and fruit, a creamy cheesecake, white meringue tarts and long caramel-glazed éclairs.

She talks softly to my mother, who had dragged me very nervously to the café through streets lined with swastika-covered red flags fluttering from gold-spired flagpoles.

A high-ranking party official, Gauleiter Wagner, is in town today, and at home she wondered whether she dared go shopping for the birthday things. On the way to the café, we had passed some Brownshirts who were pasting yellow and white posters covered with black writing on to walls and advertising pillars while their brushes dripped with glue. Instead of answering my question about what they were doing, Mother had quickened her step. And now I understand from the loud whispers of the two women that these black words may spell our doom.

The pretzels don't taste very good, and even the big round cake with "32 years" in chocolate letters doesn't manage to cheer me up. I feel like I'm trapped under a glass dome and the voices sound as if they're coming from far away.

The walk home is hampered by my self-imposed task of not missing any of the blue granite curbstones. One wrong step can bring unprecedented disaster, and just before we reach the front door, with the end in sight, I lose my balance.

Tonight is not like our usual Sabbath evenings. My grandmother prays longer and bows deeper to the East. Her hands shake so much when she lights the candles that the match goes out, and when she lays her hands on my head to say her blessings, I feel her tremble. There isn't any gefilte fish or pike tonight either, and Uncle Jacob, her brother, hasn't come because he's afraid to go out on the street.

It's quiet at the table without any guests, and Father makes fast work of the prayers.

*

The curtains in my room waft me gently to sleep. I'm awakened in the ash-blue early dawn of the first day of April by raucous drunken shouts echoing between the houses and winding their way to my room through the open window.

It's Father's birthday today, keeps running through my head, and there's something else, only I can't remember what.

I hear sounds of activity in the house, but stay in bed since it's way too early. The noises outside get louder. Boots clack to the rhythm of a march and the indistinguishable words of vaguely familiar songs resound through the street.

It's not quite light when Maria wakes me up. Since my parents have gotten up already, I don't know when to recite my birthday poem.

The breakfast table is laid with warm crispy rolls which Maria has fetched in a linen bag from the bakery next door. At Father's place, there's an extra egg and a new jar of honey, which he always pours into a hollowed-out roll.

He listens to my verse with an absentminded smile and stirs his coffee. He leaves one of the eggs untouched and hurriedly scoops the honey from the jar with his coffee spoon, spilling it on the clean tablecloth.

The telephone rings.

My father holds the receiver as if he'd like to squeeze it to a pulp and his face turns white. "I'll be right there," he says hoarsely into the phone to his brother, who has surely forgotten that besides being Saturday, today is also Father's birthday.

He says something in French to my mother, who has likewise gotten up from the table and also looks strangely pale.

It can't have anything to do with me, for they speak French when it's my bedtime and it's morning now. She asks if she can go with him, but he shakes his head no, almost angrily, throws on his dark overcoat and, without his hat or walking stick, runs out the door which Maria holds open for him.

We sit silently at the table, Grandmother, Mother, Maria and I. My grandmother says some things about the Nazis that I don't understand but which frighten me anyway. Mother screams that she should keep her mouth shut and go say her Sabbath prayers in her room instead of scaring us to death.

I want to go with her, but Maria picks me up, tries to make me laugh and brings me to my play corner, where she reads me the *Adventures of Pinocchio.*

My throat stops pounding.

In the pauses between the sentences, I hear my mother on the phone and the dull drone of marching songs against the windowpanes.

The morning creeps along in dismal slowness.

Mother says to Maria that she feels cooped up, like being stuck in the cabin of a ship during a storm; that she wants to go out, to the store, to my father. Maria hesitates, thinks it's not safe, but lets herself be talked into it. Grandmother protests, says she doesn't want to stay alone, and argues excitedly, her quarrelsome voice breaking from emotion. Mother sticks to her guns, unlike her usual self, and lets my grandmother rant and rave in her room.

Walking in between Mother and Maria, I feel insignificant today. Their hands are cold. Their fuzzy coats tickle. We trudge silently through the steep and quiet back streets where there are few people. On other Saturdays there is an outdoor market between the bare linden trees on Sophienstrasse, where plump peasant women extol the virtues of their chickens and eggs and where a monkey sometimes dances to the tunes that a tow-haired harmonica player plays on his shining Hohner. Instead, today I see a circle of people in front of Uncle Rudi's store. We hurriedly walk in back of them, and Mother squeezes my hand as if she's afraid I'll run away.

Shouted commands break the silence from time to time, and the murmured whispers of the shivering-cold onlookers sound like a response.

Between the men and women, I can vaguely see two Brownshirts, clutching poles in their hands like halberdiers. The white placards mounted on the poles are covered with words in bold black letters. On their heads, the men are wearing hard brown helmets with chinstraps. In the distance, in Leopold Square, there's a dark mass of people, with a sprinkling of brown and red uniforms. I'd like to take a look, but am held tight on either side by solicitous hands.

In the street leading to the back of Grandmother's store, I recognize Hotel Tannhäuser.

Two large windows have been broken and you can see

right inside from the road. A man who is gray all over, the owner, is sitting at the counter, speechless and still, with his eyes wide open. He doesn't seem to recognize us even though he'd recently been seated at our table at home, discussing the wedding reception of Father's cousin. He'd been in such good spirits then, and it had been a wonderful reception. After the service in the synagogue, where my father had sung an aria which moved everyone to tears and where the bridal couple had stepped on a wineglass, a long procession of elegantly clad relatives from Alsace and nearby cities and villages had crossed Sophienstrasse and poured into his hotel. Long tables had been arranged in a big square and covered with white tablecloths, floral arrangements and candelabra, with three forks and three glasses beside each plate.

My mother, in a long glittering yellow dress, was almost more beautiful than Aunt Selma in her bridal gown, whose long train I had helped carry.

I sat beside my mother and swapped jokes across the table with my cousins. Nobody paid any attention to what I ate, and time and again my plate was whisked away with leftover food I would never have dared leave on my plate at home.

My elderly uncle from Rastatt, who resembled the cows he traded in, slid his ice cream and candy over to me, and I kept on eating until I was nearly sick to my stomach. We children played underneath the table, while the uncles up above smoked fat Uppman cigars following the Grace After Meals known as benshen.

Their wives sat together and clucked like hens in a

chicken coop. My father, seated at the piano, sang his most beautiful songs, and everyone listened quietly or hummed along. Grandmother's French brother, Uncle Edward, showed me how his gold watch sprang open. It tinkled so clearly and beautifully, and I fell asleep in his lap.

Now the owner is staring into nothingness and doesn't hear my mother when she asks him through the broken and paint-smeared window what actually happened.

Full of anxious foreboding, we quicken our pace, spurred on by Mother's agitation.

At the bottom of the street, where long ago the Romans drank from hot springs and where the steaming water still patters into a rocky fountain, we turn off in the direction of Grandmother's furniture store. I can already see a lot of people, many more than usual, and I don't understand what they're doing there. Mother's hard grip hurts my hand.

From on high, the gray knight Bismarck, with his sword and spiked helmet, looks impassively down on us, and my vague suspicions are confirmed by the sight before us.

We thread our way to the front through the onlookers. Some are scowling, others look resigned or upset. But some are grinning as if the spectacle is providing them with a great deal of pleasure. One of these is Mr. Kindler from the clothing store on the corner. He's standing in the front row, his legs wide, his hands at his sides, the gleaming-red pin with the swastika on his leather jacket.

Huge men in the brown uniform of the Stormtroopers are positioned on either side of the doorway with their revolvers strapped to their Sam Browne belts and their legs encased in shiny black boots. They are standing as still as statues. Beside them, mounted on poles, are large placards with words I can understand even though I can't read. Rowdy boys, heads taller than I am, shout the slogans, while the adults, in their musty worn-out clothes mutter their approval or nod their heads in agreement. "Don't buy from Jews, they will be your downfall" and "Jews are ruining the nation. Germans, put a stop to this now!" Stars of David have been scrawled on the broad store windows with whitewash, dripping towards the corners in long white streaks and ruining the beautiful new black marble frame.

A tall broad-shouldered man with brown hair and dirty hands, the head mechanic at the garage where Father parks his car, squeezes his way to the front like we did. He tries to reach the door to the store by passing through the Brownshirts, but one of them stretches out his arm and blocks the way. The Brownshirt snaps at him: "Can't you read, you stupid Jew-lover? We'll have to teach this guy a lesson." No voice is raised in his defense and no one protests.

He leaves without saying a word, his shoulders stooped, his back bowed.

My mother doesn't dare take another step. The other Stormtrooper notices us and says with a gesture of mock servility: "Do go in, Madam, we'll be glad to relieve you of your money." And he flashes Maria a phoney smile: "And we'll see to you shortly."

Under dozens of averted heads or mocking faces feigning cold indifference, we reach the paint-smeared door with our hearts pounding and our shoes seemingly full of lead. Mr. Kindler greets us with a nasty grin and I feel sick with fear.

The showroom is deserted and cold. Light is shining in the office behind the rolls of linoleum.

My aunt and uncle are sitting in the office in their good Sabbath clothes. My father brusquely snaps at my mother that she shouldn't have come. She bursts into tears and Gersbach tries to offer her comfort and support. He says that everything will turn out all right and I take his word for it.

Racked with sobs, my mother tells the story of what happened outside, in front of the door. My aunt's eyes look furious through her thick glasses. She hisses what appears to be a swear word in Dutch and disappears into the washroom in her good dress. Swathed in an apron and armed with a bucket, cloth and sponge, she strides between the armchairs and beds and, without saying a word to anyone, throws open the door. Uncle Benno, his whiny voice breaking, orders her to stop: "Jet, come back, you can't do that here." But she continues, unruffled, on her way.

She washes the dirtied store windows with the wet rag and sponge, gaped at by the dumbfounded and cow-eyed bystanders.

A Brownshirt shouts something at her, tries to kick over her bucket. She looks him right in the eye and unleashes a raging torrent of Dutch on him.

He stares at her in incomprehension and doesn't know what to do with himself when she suddenly changes languages and snaps at him that she "will be informing the Dutch ambassador of this."

The onlookers move off as if the spectacle fails to hold their interest. Only a few lanky youths continue to hang around.

In the washroom, where she fills the bucket with clean water and washes the white gunk off her hands, she nods satisfied and self-assured: "That's how we do things in Holland."

DROWNING

Every time my mirrored, wood-paneled, rust-brown compartment passes a floor and a door glides by, the wrought-iron grille makes a loud click. I go up and down from basement to attic, and only the button-studded red uniform and flat cap of the real elevator boy would make my joy complete. I operate the buttons as I have seen him do in the elevator located in another part of the hotel, and I no longer feel the cross boredom that had plagued me at the table of my parents and their acquaintances. Nobody at the table had said anything to me, and the words I overheard awakened the forgotten fears I had felt a year earlier when the men with the brown shirts and the red swastika-emblazoned armbands had painted slogans on the display windows of our store. Though the whispered names and terms of abuse were familiar to me, the conversation remained obscure. Even my mother joined in, her cheeks red, and forgot that I was sitting there. No one stopped me when I left the spacious high-ceilinged room where wisps of smoke from the talking mouths of dozens of grownups rose to the ceiling like storm clouds and where waiters with flapping tails danced trays full of coffee cups and glasses of red, green and yellow drinks on their hands without spilling a drop.

Behind the tall, smooth, gleaming counter, hundreds of numbered boxes are filled with letters, newspapers and keys dangling from numbered plates. I don't pass by unseen, for the fat bald man in the moss-green uniform who wanted to shake my hand when we arrived and asked me my name says in his funny German that I mustn't get lost.

I saunter slowly through the long corridors and look at the pictures of deer, dogs and birds hanging on the walls. In a new and unfamiliar long corridor with a slightly worn runner, I see an elevator which has the same curly lattice-work gate as the one in our corridor. My mother hasn't let me operate the buttons alone or close the two doors. She's afraid my fingers will get caught, even though I can operate our elevator at home with the best of them.

The rattling rides from basement to attic and from attic to basement don't hold my attention for long, and when I press a button to stop, my cage remains suspended between floors. Neither pulling on the inside door nor playing with the buttons makes the car move. What seemed so friendly at first now seems downright hostile. I feel trapped, and my wide-eyed image stares back anxiously at me from the mirrors.

The fear that I will die here, alone and miserable, creeps up on me like a snake, for in spite of my cry for help and my loud wails no one comes to rescue me.

I wake with a start at the metallic rattling of my cage and

see above me the shoes and legs of my parents and the green trouser legs of the head doorman. My pants are cold and wet. My embarrassment prevails over my fear of punishment as I'm walked past the curious grownups to our hotel room in Merano.

Late in the morning of the next day, as the pale-blue mist lifts over the vineyards, we discover Merano's swimming pool: long rows of pink cubicles, colorful reclining chairs, various-sized pools, and a children's playground that draws me like a magnet.

Even though there are no signs anywhere forbidding entrance to Jews, like we have at home, my mother still stammers shyly at the man behind the cash register.

Inside, my parents quickly recognize friends from the high-ceilinged dining room, and they resume their twittering conversation as if they hadn't been interrupted by the night.

The sing-song call of the ice-cream vendor, "Gelati, gelati," drowns out the excited talk and wakes me from my playground reverie.

Sitting on the back seat of our dark-blue Adler, my father's spotless pride and joy, I sleepily watch the mountainous landscape pass me by. On long straight stretches, when the car is quietly humming along, he pushes his white traveling cap to the back of his head and sings at the top of his lungs. My mother chimes in, and two-part arias fill the car more freely and cheerfully than in our music room at home.

The route along Lake Garda chases away any thoughts of

sleep. I shudder with pleasure in the eerie, roughly hewn tunnels we keep disappearing into, and squeeze my eyes shut in the white sunlight at the end of each tunnel.

Every time I open my eyes again, the landscape is different. Only the deep-blue sea, the gray- and pink-veined rocks and the white triangles of the sailboats stay the same. Sometimes my father stops the car at a vista point and snaps a picture or lets me look through the binoculars at a faraway marble quarry, village or mountain. Though I seldom see anything he points out through the binoculars, I don't say anything, because I don't want to miss my chance to hold that beautiful black object.

Riva is where we're heading for on our vacation, and after adjusting the focus and having been helped to locate the view, I see the pink, blue and sea-green houses along its waterfront; the small harbor and jetty, with a flag-bedecked ferry boat docked at the landing; the hotel terraces, with awnings jutting out over the windows like melon halves; the people sitting at white tables under gaily striped umbrellas; and the sailboats dancing on their ropes.

In less than an hour we belong to Riva, and the owner of the gelateria across from our hotel has conjured up three colorful sundaes, scooping the ice cream out of deep canisters whose white metal lids look like pointed hats.

The weeks that follow are both monotonous and varied.

The walks to Torbole along the highway in oppressive heat: my father in the lead, with his walking stick, knickerbockers, white cap and polo shirt. My mother behind me, balancing on thin-soled high heels, calls to him to slow his pace a little. On the beach, the bathers are wearing broad-stripe swimming suits. My mother's chin-strapped rubber bathing cap transforms her into a strange creature from the deep.

I play with sand and pebbles. Sometimes we toss a rubber ring back and forth, but I'm usually left to entertain myself. Like me, the other children stick close to their parents, and I look enviously at families with several children. How wonderful it would be to have a playmate.

My father goes splashing and spluttering into the water and emerges from it like a snorting sea monster. I dare to go with him a few yards, but when the cold wetness reaches my waist, even his outstretched hand doesn't reassure me.

When the sun shines, we often sit under the umbrellas lining the harbor, and sometimes the wind blows my mother's dark brown hair loose. Time and again, she sticks a hairpin into it, but sooner or later it falls out, and then I hunt around for it.

A lot happens in that harbor. The paddle steamer, which I'm familiar with from a ride we took on the lake and whose groaning, monstrous metal arms in the open hold afforded me more pleasure than the panoramas admired by everyone on the deck, brings dozens of vacationers, villagers and soldiers with every arrival. The squawking tourists alight on the terraces around us. The other passengers disappear behind the row of houses.

Once I watch breathlessly as an endless line of boys, some of them not much taller than I am, wearing dark shirts and kepis and red scarves around their necks, come singing from the gangplank. They stand, aligned in rows, at the water's edge and then march singing to the jetty. Once there, they keep on singing, beating drums and blowing small flutes. Waiters, guests and townspeople hurry to the spot. We stay in our seats, along with my parents' newly acquired friends, even though I desperately want to go watch. "It's the Balilla", my father whispers in my ear, and I guess what that means.

The tall waiter, Herr Fritz, who has big ears and blond hair combed stiffly to the side and who always walks around in tails, even when the other waiters are only wearing vests, sometimes points out beautiful ships on the lake, asks me about my home, my dog Senta or what I want to be when I grow up and often brings me a crayon, a balloon or a piece of drawing paper along with my ice cream. He doesn't say much, but I know he's my friend.

Only a few days of our vacation are left. After a long, difficult climbing trip to the marble quarry, we return sticky with sweat and dust to our customary table on our usual terrace, but it's sultry and humid here too. Pearly-gray clouds are gathering over the lake, and it's busier and noisier in the harbor than usual. Radio voices, German and Italian, ring out from open windows.

Men are standing together in groups, listening to loudspeakers and then resuming their noisy conversations.

A paddle steamer is moored to the landing. The air turns purple, and the wind blows white summer hats across the cobblestones.

A couple with two boys, one about six years old like me and the other maybe eight, comes directly from the gangplank to the table in front of ours. The two boys are wearing white shirts. I watch in envy as they spoon up the enormous dishes of ice cream Herr Fritz serves them, and I don't feel an ounce of sympathy when their mother angrily explodes at them for spilling on their clean clothes.

Their parents get into a conversation with my parents, and suddenly it's as if the grownups on the terrace are all talking to each other at the same time. Lost and bored among all the agitated adults, I hear the jabbering voices, the blaring loudspeakers, the rumble of distant thunder, and I look longingly at the two boys, who are standing at the end of the landing pulling a boat on a string through the water.

Shyness and fear of that immense stretch of water keep me rooted to my chair.

Gusts of wind tear at the awnings and umbrellas. Dancing ships with their sails reefed grind against the jetty and tug at their lines like dogs on a leash.

Fascinated, I watch the two boys try to catch their toy boat, which has broken loose. The boy my age is standing at the edge crying. His mouth opens in screams but no sounds can be heard. The next moment he's disappeared from view and I can only see the brother, lying on his stomach bending over the edge. Then he too disappears.

No one seems to notice anything. In the grip of a suffocating fear, I call for help but nobody pays me the slightest bit of attention. The grownups are all listening intently to the metallic voice on the loudspeakers, snatches of which are born away by the whistling wind.

I point frantically at the empty landing, but no one understands me. Then I start screaming too, and am pushed aside as a nuisance when I pluck at sleeves. I run on to the landing and see the older boy thrashing around in the water and, further away, the hands of the younger one sticking out above the lake's surface.

Herr Fritz is standing listening to the loudspeakers with his back to the lake. I yank on his tails as if they were a bell rope and I point and point, screaming mutely in my nightmare.

He sees what I see, flings off his tailcoat and jumps without a word into the wind-whipped lake. He fights with the water, drags the unharmed older boy to safety and looks for the place where the hands of the younger have disappeared.

My parents and the other grownups appear to emerge from their stupor, throng to the water's edge and call out instructions. Looking through the forest of legs, I see a dripping Herr Fritz in a limp and rumpled dress shirt kneeling behind the boy my age, whose arms are being spread and folded like wings to bring him back to life, and the dam of my tears bursts open.

Slowly the bad dream fades away. The metallic voice from the loudspeakers is silent, the wind tempers its whistling and the squabbling of the grownups subsides.

Staring into space and sobbing from time to time, I sit between my parents. Is the younger boy alive or is that death? His bluish-white face keeps creeping back into my thoughts, along with the image of Herr Fritz pumping his arms.

I'm aroused with a start from my reverie when I hear my parents and the other guests applauding. Herr Fritz comes toward us, wearing an immaculate dress suit. Not a wrinkle anywhere. His dress shirt is stiff and clean, and his hair has been combed smooth again with a straight part. He stops in front of me, bends forward, pats me on the head and says: "The boy is alive, fortunately" and says to my parents: "The Nazis have shot Dolfuss."

Abruptly terminating our vacation days ahead of schedule, we head home. Patches of fog are drifting over the lake and the umbrella of our white table is still dripping sadly in the early-morning dew when I look shiveringly from the back seat of the Adler at the necks of my parents. They seem to be bowed. No song pours forth from their throats as on the way down here. Nowhere is it warm and safe.

MARIA AND LENA

"Don't look," says Maria, shoving her hip against my mother's to block my view of the cage.

By standing on tiptoe and craning my neck, I can see what's happened in the oval between them. Behind the brass bars of the birdcage, a tiny pile of yellow feathers with stiffly outstretched legs is lying in the birdseed on the bottom of the tray.

I can't say a word, and tears tickle my cheeks as if they aren't mine.

Then they open the screen of their bodies, and I see that the porcelain food and water bowls which I may clean and fill daily have been left untouched. I know what being ill means, but Maria explains with tears in her eyes that being dead means never getting better. My mother strokes my hair. Her nose and eyes are red and her words of comfort sound as if she has a cold.

Maria eases my grief by promising to give Hansel a real burial underneath a beautiful linden tree, just as it should be. While she looks in the sewing room for scraps of wool and black velvet, my mother finds a nice big cigar box which still smells of wood and tobacco, and I color in the most beautiful bird in my coloring book so that Hansel will have a companion. His velvet bed is awaiting him on the white marble kitchen table top, and Maria carefully and gently lays his little yellow body in it, together with my drawing.

Senta, my black German shepherd, isn't allowed to go with us today, and she understands why when I squat down in front of her basket in the hall and tell her.

Given the serious nature of our walk, Maria has donned a dark raincoat over her Dirndl, and the wide-brimmed hat with the red cherries looks very elegant on her soft brown hair, which she sometimes allows me to braid. I hold tightly to her right hand and she carries the tiny casket before her in her left hand.

We walk past the wild, bubbling waters of the Murg in the direction of the park by the Spa, avoiding the big murals outside the Pump Room since we both think these are creepy and scary.

On Michaelsberg, the hill behind the building with the hot springs, old people with canes pass us by, step by step. We are spoken to twice by inquisitive ladies with wrinkled faces who have gold pendants on black ribbons tied around their necks. Maria explains what we're doing and, nodding gravely, they allow us to continue.

Out of breath at the top of the hill, we look down below. Maria points out our house, far beneath us in the valley, and assures me that my mother is standing on the lookout. She wipes my forehead with her handkerchief, which smells of eau de cologne.

At the top of Michaelsberg, we hunt a little furtively for a nice spot between the old linden trees. Maria draws my sand shovel from her coat pocket, and we take turns digging a hole under a bush in a place no one else knows.

Hansel's coffin fits in it, and when the wooden box has disappeared under the soil I realize I'll never see my bird again. My eyes fill with tears, and through the tears I see that Maria's eyes are also moist.

She lays two sticks in the form of a cross on top of the mound of earth and then takes my head between her dirt-encrusted hands, plants a kiss on my forehead and says softly, "May God protect you, Gerdl."

Her words make me unutterably sad, without knowing exactly why. A big sob is stuck in my chest and throat, and my mother, hearing the hoarseness in my voice when I'm back home, asks me if I've caught cold, up there on the hilltop.

The days that follow are gray rain clouds dripping half-understood sentences. Maria has been summoned by the "Gestapo." The Brownshirts have been to see her parents. At the table she tells of angry men who have derided and threatened her. With a lump in her throat, she reads aloud a letter from her father, in which he asks her to come home. Maria wants to stay. My mother holds a tear-stained handkerchief in her hand. My father predicts danger and stutters now and again. Maria's fear resonates in me. I throw my arms around her neck to keep her by me.

She'll think of me, of Senta and of my parents a whole lot. She'll write to us often, she promises in a whisper, and all this trouble will soon be over.

The next morning, two large rust-colored Mädler suitcases, trimmed in brass and wood and fitted with brass locks, are waiting in the hall when I surreptitiously steal out of my bed. Barefoot and nightshirted, I touch the objects of doom and feel how heavy they are. Against my better judgement, I hope the luggage won't fit in the car, that Maria will change her mind and say with a laugh, "I'll stay." What keeps running through my head is: "Oh don't go, stay with me!"

The summer sun is shining as Maria climbs into the car beside my father. The suitcases are on the back seat, with her dark raincoat and cherry hat on top. She smiles at me through her tears, and I wave and wave until she drowns in the sea of my sorrows.

Without Maria, our house is empty and unfriendly. The heavy dark furniture frowns forbiddingly and the grand piano gleams, black and unapproachable.

The heavy green vacuum-cleaner sled that I tote around behind my mother groans and whines. Despite the red kerchief on her head, a lock of hair keeps falling over her heated face, which she brushes back with her hand. She doesn't say much while she's doing the cleaning, nor later on in the kitchen. Senta's tail droops sadly, even when she's allowed to go shopping with us. My tiny gray-haired grandmother, wearing her wobbly pince-nez, long black dress and crocheted shawl, sits for hours every day at her new treadle sewing machine, mending or making over clothes which I have to try on with the prickly pins still in them. After Maria's departure, Grandmother came to live with us for good and had her room wallpapered in dark green and brown stripes. The corner containing her huge mahogany bed looks like a burrow. The fresh scent of eau de cologne and wild flowers has been dispelled by valerian drops and camphor.

In the morning and late afternoon, I sometimes see her reciting her prayers from a book. Nodding her head and swaying her torso, she stands in front of the blank wall facing east and doesn't respond when I ask a question or make a remark.

When it's raining or I'm bored, I race my wind-up train through her room or make a hut out of her camel-hair blanket and two chairs. Then she talks of her youth in Alsace; her apprenticeship as a dressmaker in Strasbourg; Uncle Edward in Metz with his wet gray mustache and bowler hat who fought so bravely in Verdun; her other surviving brothers and sisters living safely in France; and the village near Kehl where she was born, which I know from boring Sunday visits.

On Saturdays she prays longer than usual and wears her elegant black dress with the white lace collar and jabot. She doesn't want to go to the synagogue, since she no longer dares to go outside where Nazis roam the streets.

Her arrival has changed our Friday evenings. The silver Sabbath candelabra which belonged to my mother's father are set out on the gleaming white damask tablecloth as usual. But the gold-rimmed Rosenthal dishes which used to be tucked away in the buffet now shine like new under the wide silk bell lamp. My grandmother blesses the candles, murmurs a prayer and holds her hands over the flames as if she wants to warm herself. The black Eden hat is perched on my father's head; I feel uncomfortable under my cloth cap. We are all dressed in our very best. My father sings as we stand at our plates, and I have to repeat incomprehensible Hebrew words over a piece of egg bread covered with poppy seeds and salt and sip sweet wine from a pockmarked silver chalice.

After chicken soup, my mother goes to the kitchen to fetch a platter of green carp floating in brown or green aspic. It turns my stomach, but I feel obliged to taste it out of courtesy to my grandmother, who is proud of her culinary efforts.

My Uncle Jacob, Grandmother's favorite brother, a regular Friday guest at our table, sometimes eats half a fish. He's poor and complains constantly about money and rheumatism. Sometimes he leads the Grace After Meals and drags it out so long that my parents and I yawn with boredom.

If he's restless and jumpy and leaves the grace to my father and nervously opens and shuts the lid of his heavy pocket watch, I know only too well what will follow after dinner. The magic word "Bayreuth" reduces everyone to silence. Uncle Jacob and my father drag heavy armchairs over to the new Blaupunkt Superhet cabinet radio, and before long *The Valkyrie, The Meistersinger* or the voice of Elsa von Brabant are booming through the dining room. With one hand cupped behind his ear so as not to miss a note, my uncle sits directly in front of the speaker and angrily shushes anyone who makes a sound clearing the table, opens a door or whispers a word.

Wagner, whose bronze bust adorns our grand piano, is our household god.

A few days after my father has left on a business trip, my grandmother takes to her bed.

Dr. Roos, our elderly family doctor, has a head that shines like an Easter egg, gold-rimmed glasses on the tip of his nose and large red hands which hurt me once during an office visit, when he pressed on my stomach. He stays with her a long time. As he leaves, he pinches my cheek too hard and says I mustn't bother my grandmother.

My hope of spending some pleasant days alone with my mother fades when I see that Grandmother requires her constant attention. She has to be helped to sit up or lie down, or she wants water, soup or coffee in a special cup, and the clanking white bedpan has to be fetched and carried continuously. I help with the dusting, but am reproved when I do something wrong. My mother is sad and dejected and I feel helpless and irritable.

In her pink, crocheted bed jacket, my grandmother sits enthroned amid the plump feather pillows piled against the beautifully grained headboard of her bed. Her hair, which my mother combs and brushes every morning, is hanging around her shoulders. She's busy crocheting a new bed jacket, as if she expects to be bedridden a long time. She complains long and frequently, even though she's making marked improvement.

She rarely leaves her bed, and she argues with the doctor when he tries to persuade her to get up. I start playing again on the rug in her room with my train, Meccano set and recently acquired Mickey Mouse, who flails his arms and walks when I wind him up with a little key in his back. When you pick him up, he treads the air with his black feet and shakes his head from side to side, going clickety-click faster than the sewing machine. When you hold him in your hand, it's as if he's alive and trying to escape.

My grandmother is sleeping under her eiderdown like Little Red Riding Hood's grandmother.

In the hilly area formed by the sheets, I give my Mickey Mouse free rein. Grandmother's eyes open wide in surprise and her toothless baby mouth tries to form words. Instead, she suddenly crows like a hoarse rooster, recoils in fright and starts beating wildly at my toy. She shrieks my mother's name, and in my confusion, fright and indignation I grab the kicking creature and plunk it down on top of her head. It slowly thrashes around until it gets entangled in her gray locks, and the screaming continues unabated.

My world collapses as my mother is forced to use a pair of scissors to extricate the convulsing Mickey Mouse from the tangle of gray. Out of breath, my grandmother hisses that I'm a mamzer, a devil, and she swears that I won't be let off without punishment. My mother seems on the verge of tears. She tries to calm my grandmother, pours a few valerian drops in a glass of water and sends me from the room.

Sore with sorrow and pain after the harsh punishment meted out by my father, I lie that evening in my bed with an empty stomach and a pounding head. His bellows can be heard from the dining room, and my mother sobs and shouts that, without Maria, she can't continue to bear the burden alone.

A few days later, we hurry home from shopping. Lena, Mother's new cleaning lady, is coming to introduce herself. I'm bursting with impatience and curiosity to see her. The outside door leading to the staircase is ajar. Even downstairs, I can hear Senta's excited barks.

I run ahead of my mother up the smooth flagstone steps to our second-floor apartment, but stop short when I see through the banister that Lena is stamping her man-sized black lace-up boots on the floor to get the dog to shut up.

She only notices us when we're standing beside her. The nose of our now softly whimpering German shepherd is visible through the panes in the white door.

Before saying hello and introducing herself, Lena snarls that we should hold the dog tight when the door is opened.

Mother nervously inserts the key in the lock and sternly orders Senta to her basket, where she keeps a watchful, wary eye on our new cleaning lady.

When it's my turn to shake Lena's mammoth purple hand, I feel a deep bond with my dog. This big coarse female, with a pointed nose and lackluster eyes that pierce right through you, is downright creepy. Her graying brown hair has been pulled into a thick hairpin-studded bun at the nape of her neck, and I can't keep my eyes off the hairs on her chin. I sense that Mother is also shocked, but she allows Lena to start work right away. Lena pulls a big brown apron from a wicker suitcase, and after exchanging only a few words, starts dusting and polishing as if the house belongs to her.

My mother busies herself with the cooking and doesn't allow anyone or anything to budge her from the stove. When we're seated around the table, my father sniggers softly that he's glad "that hag" prefers to eat in the kitchen. We all whisper a lot in our house now, for Lena listens at doors. Until I saw her race through the hall with my own eyes once when Father jerked open the door, I couldn't believe that grownups would do such a thing.

Recriminations can be heard from the kitchen, but we keep on whispering anyway. During the week, my grandmother rarely emerges from her room, and when she does, she shuffles silently past Lena.

Gradually Grandmother stops being angry at me. Seated on chairs beside her bed or the sewing machine, which she sets to whirring again from time to time, we pour out our hearts to each other. It's as if our apartment has been taken over by a dragon, and my father is the only one who dares to take it on.

When I see plump peasant women with baskets of bluish oval plums in the market behind the Catholic Collegiate Church, I know my mother is going to start baking. She layers the pitted plum halves in long rows on top of the dough in oblong baking tins and sprinkles them with sugar, cinnamon and light cream. This she does deftly and with a great deal of pleasure.

The plum tart is still warm and juicy when she lets us

taste the first pieces. Lena looks almost friendly as she stuffs a double helping into her mouth.

My eyes bigger than my stomach, I ask for more. But my mother replies that guests are coming to dinner tomorrow, Friday evening. She carefully sets aside a platter heaped with extra nice crustless pieces in the pantry off the kitchen.

Uncle Jacob's face clouds over in the hall when he hears that Mother's plump sister and her boyfriend Harry, the actor with the monocle, and even Uncle Albert, Father's second cousin, are coming to dine tonight. He fears and I hope that Wagner won't stand a chance after dinner.

My father is more devout than usual and sings the prayers as if they're arias. I wait quietly at the festively decorated table for the plum tart. There's no need to eat the carp in their green sheaths today, since my aunt also leaves her portion untouched.

My mother calls me from the kitchen with a catch in her voice. Unaware of any wrongdoing, except my dislike of the fish, I go to the kitchen and see her standing in tears beside the tart platter, which has been reduced from a mountain to a gentle slope. I stand there as the accused, even though I know I'm absolutely innocent this time. She only believes me after I've sworn an everlasting oath. Her cross-examination also extends to my father, who knows nothing about it and starts to fume. Grandmother is above all suspicion. That leaves Lena as the sole suspect, and she's not due back until Monday morning.

The sharp, shrill sounds of an altercation rise up to the apartment from the laundry room in the basement via the hollow stairwell and I know, without being able to make out the words, what it's about. Flustered and pale, her eyes rimmed with red, my mother storms into the living room and breathlessly trips over her words: Lena has stolen the tart, and what's worse, Lena has been pilfering the pantry for quite some time. But even worse than that, Lena swears and scoffs that she's entitled, that we're exploiting her and giving her too little to eat, that the Jews are a menace to the "German nation" and that she's going to send the Nazi Party down on us to teach us a lesson once and for all.

Tart, canned goods, sausages and cheese instantly fade into insignificance. Anger turns to fear, and I can already imagine the Brownshirts standing at the door with their torchlights and clubs. At their wit's end, my parents consult each other, their friends and their circle of acquaintances. The telephone dial goes click-click all day long and my mother breathlessly relates her story into the phone. That evening, she calls on the neighbors living upstairs and to the left and right of us.

Exhausted and wound to a fever pitch, she gives me a goodnight kiss. My curiosity smoldering, I fall asleep with the comforting tip of the pillow in my arms.

The next morning, Lena whisks surly and tight-lipped through the house. The pots and pans in the kitchen jangle angrily and she acts as if we aren't even there. She kicks harder at chair and table legs than I would ever have dared in one of my worst temper tantrums, and when I hear the dull thuds of the carpets being beaten in the courtyard, I feel sorry for the carpets.

*

My mother cooks lunch. Her cheeks are flushed as if the kitchen is sweltering, and she winces every time she hears a bang or thud inside or outside the apartment.

I help her set the table in silence, and when the soup is steaming in its tureen on the table, she calls Lena to come and eat.

Mother gently shuts the kitchen door and leaves the soup-slurping Lena, whose gaze is concentrated on the food, to her fate. We eat our soup without a word, and I don't understand what the expectant silence means.

When the doorbell rings, my mother jumps up like a jack-in-the-box, runs to the front door and returns a moment later with a mysterious troop of tiptoeing, whispering ladies. In their fore is Mrs. Huber, our blonde, well-rounded, ever-smiling upstairs neighbor, wearing a green Dirndl with a gold cross nestled in her ample bosom.

The women are standing either in the hall or halfway in the living room when Mrs. Huber throws open the kitchen door. Lena doesn't even deign to glance at her. Her left arm is curved around her plate as if to ward off attackers. Her right hand is wrapped around a fork, which she's using to shovel huge bites of sauerkraut, meat and potatoes into her mouth from the mound on her plate, without raising her arm.

Our upstairs neighbor and the other ladies have all filed into the kitchen by the time the distracted Lena looks up from her food. Mrs. Huber's laughing words: "But Lena, I thought they were starving you here" brings the fork to a standstill. A thundercloud passes over her face, and her lips thin into a tight crack. Muttering, she stands up, clamps the fork in her fist like a hayfork and jabs it in the middle of the sauerkraut. She looks around scowling, spews out a series of oaths I've never heard before, snatches her brown apron from the hook and without pausing to stuff it into the wicker suitcase, shoves us away from the kitchen door. She slams the front door behind her with a resounding bang. Her malediction echoes in the hollow stairwell: "Drop dead, you Jews!"

Pale, the merriment erased from their faces, the women shuffle outside. My mother's whispered words of thanks hang heavy in the air.

SCHOOLDAYS

I hardly recognize myself any more in the hall mirror and I'm almost on the verge of tears. Only the top of my head still has some hair left, for the barber has applied his grating clippers to the back and sides and turned me into a porcupine. "It has to be short and smart for school," he tells my mother. And without allowing her time to reconsider or wasting another word on the subject, he gives me a German haircut. Brown locks fall on the white hairdressing cape like autumn leaves, and I shut my tear-filled eyes to avoid having to watch my transformation.

On the way home, I feel the cold wind on my shorn head, and it suddenly seems as if my cap has gotten too big for me. A boy in my neighborhood named Harro, the son of the head mechanic at the Opel garage where Father parks his car, makes a beeline for us on his scooter. His hair has been similarly cropped recently. I feel sure he's laughing at me because my cap is too big, even though he's usually so nice. I tug at Mother's hand in order to reach the stairwell, where

I'm safe from the gaze of strangers, and only rest easy when the front door shuts behind us.

She lures me away from the hall mirror with a rustling surprise wrapped in brown paper. The broad dining-room table is covered with a gray linen tablecloth which my grandmother, muttering with effort, has spent months embroidering with flowers, her bespectacled nose nearly touching the cloth with every stitch. She shrieks from her armchair that the new tablecloth should be folded away before I may be allowed to untie the strings on the package. I can smell the exhilarating odor of newly tanned leather through the paper, and with impatient fingers I remove the brown wrapping from the most beautiful school satchel I've ever laid hands on.

Speechless, I stroke the magnificent crinkly leather, follow the smooth rectangular shape of the flap with my index finger and stick my head in the bag to inhale its pungent aroma. A long wooden pencil box is resting on the bottom. I only manage to open its mysterious lock after a great deal of searching and poking around. No one in the room comes up with the idea of first pulling out the sliding lid halfway.

The box lies heavy and smooth in my hand, a massive chunk of wood. Colored pencils and a fountain pen rattle around inside. Extra nibs with bulbous points, a small chamois and a soft green eraser have been tucked away in a secret compartment.

The leather shoulder straps on my satchel are stiff and hard. I need help clasping the right strap to the metal ring underneath the bag, but after a few abortive attempts I finally get the hang of it. I walk proudly from the room in my new school gear and survey myself in the hall mirror through other, new eyes.

I had often passed by the glistening graystone school building with my parents or holding Maria's hand on the way to see my friend Walter, the son of the fat rabbi, or on the occasional Sundays that we rode the groaning cable car to the top of Merkur Mountain.

Dozens of mothers, with boys my size or bigger whose hair has been cropped like mine, are standing on the gray granite staircase leading up from the sidewalk or on the broad landing between the balustrade and the school's menacing arched entryway. While some of the boys are carrying leather or canvas schoolbags, others have linen bags or bundles tied with string. In their arms they're cradling large cones fashioned out of colored silk, cardboard or brown paper and filled with brightly wrapped candies, Easter eggs and chocolates. They shout back and forth, brag about their Easter goodies and swap their treats.

Some of the mothers are jabbering noisily with other mothers while their youngsters hang from the balustrade or dirty their Easter clothes.

Walter and I stand without a cone of candy on the sidewalk across from the school. Our mothers talk in nearly inaudible whispers and we explore each other's schoolbags. His ears stick out and turn red when he looks at the Easter candy, and I too am consumed by envy.

In booming voices the teachers order the boys to line up

in three rows, and we hurry up the steps clutching our mothers' hands to join the end of the line. A photographer with a large tripod-mounted camera threads his way through the crowd and disappears inside. Mothers, teachers and pupils are swallowed up in the school's dark maw.

We are the last in line, and a tall thin man with a wreath of graying hair around his bald pate is waiting in the doorway for us. His mustache resembles a brush. A pair of round spectacles are clamped to his shiny nose. He bows awkwardly in my mother's direction, shakes her hand and introduces himself as the head teacher, Mr. Kreis. Then, fumbling for words, he asks my mother and Walter's mother to return to school later in the day or even tomorrow, school pictures being such a problem these days . . . Jewish children . . . Sie verstehen . . . We walk down the steps and say goodbye to each other almost without exchanging a word. I walk mutely alongside my mother, the pencil box rattling in my schoolbag.

Out of all the eyes staring at us I recognize only the face of Harro. Walter and I remain standing at the classroom door. While our mothers are talking softly to Mr. Kreis, we're being examined by the class like alien fish in a fishbowl. The two empty seats are far away from each other, with Walter at the head of the first row and me halfway down the last one, next to the window. I can only see a little bit of the back of his head. We're not allowed to sit beside each other.

Harro rescues me from my loneliness and asks if he may change places with the unfamiliar boy next to me who had sized me up with a hostile glance when I was seated beside him. In his new Lederhosen and genuine Haferl shoes, he strides proudly to Harro's desk as if he's glad to have nothing more to do with us.

Our mothers vanish into the hall and a fearful sense of abandonment makes my knees weak. Harro is scant comfort. The sullen cropped heads of my classmates, the towering graying teacher whose stern gaze sees everything, the bamboo cane in the corner, the strange upright letters on the blackboard which don't resemble the ones my grandmother had taught me at home: an unknown world fraught with danger.

During the lunch break, the boys swap sandwiches with each other, but not with me. In the bathroom, where we have to line up in adjacent rows and pee against a black wall, we inspect each other's genitals and I discover how I'm different from boys of another religion and how they're different from me.

Stories of punishments meted out with swishing bamboo canes race through the corridors like thunderclouds, but Mr. Kreis never touches his cane. Now and again a child is made to stand in the corner for making too much noise or teasing someone, but Mr. Kreis is never really unkind. I gradually begin to feel less insecure. He doesn't allow the others to ridicule us or call us names and he maintains order in the classroom.

I learn the bold upright letters quickly and, with my tongue between my lips, I do my sums without making any errors. From time to time I surreptitiously help Harro, but am sent to the corner once when Mr. Kreis catches me.

Early every morning, I walk past the old peeling houses on long, hollow Stephanienstrasse with Maria at my side. We usually wait for Harro, who emerges at a run from the garage's big door. We then hop and skip ahead of her, and she has trouble keeping up with us. We take her hand as we go by the high school, for the big boys at that school, dressed in uniforms with leather Sam Browne belts and swastika armbands, look as menacing as a pack of wolves.

If we hear the screech of the lathe or the dull thuds of the anvil coming from the blacksmith's, we stick our heads around the corner of the workshop door and say hello to Harro's uncle, who is the boss there. In a deep rolling voice, he wishes his nephew a good day at school and nods to me as if I really belong.

Maria remains standing at the foot of the school's stone steps and waves to us as we're being led through the big door in orderly rows of three.

Although a few of my classmates give me a faint hello, most of them look right through me. The boys around Fritz with the Lederhosen turn their heads away. Mr. Kreis had punished them for tripping Walter and me, and afterwards they had called us kikes.

We slam down the wooden seats with the squealing hinges, slide into our desks and unpack our notebooks and pencil boxes from our nearly empty satchels or pockets.

Then the head of our teacher can be seen through the windowpanes in the classroom door. Even before the door is fully open, the entire class jumps to attention beside the desks. After he's reached his lectern, all the boys except Walter and me raise their right arms and shout in unison "Heil Hitler, Teacher Sir."

He merely raises his hand, palm outward, and mumbles "Heil Hitler" too, as if in thanks.

The class had practiced for weeks to be able to perform this feat in chorus, but Mr. Kreis had said to me, in a low whisper, that I wasn't obliged to make the Hitler salute. I do sing along with the songs, albeit not at the top of my voice. I hum the malevolent words and feign ignorance, as if I don't understand how they can have anything to do with us.

I talk to Harro during recess, and our paths only part outside the garage door. His uncle, the blacksmith, is a beacon of safety on our way home.

My father is rarely home. He travels far away with huge suitcases full of print tablecloths and curtain samples. Now that he no longer has the store, I never see him on weekdays. The brief postcards he writes in his bold hand merely say whether business is good or bad and indicate to my mother in a kind of secret language what his volume of trade was that day or week. On the Saturdays and Sundays that he's home, we go out. We ride the cable car in which you can sit upright even though it's built on a slant, while the heavy black cable pulls you higher and higher to the top of the Merkur. We're often accompanied by friends of my parents, who never bring along a playmate for me. I'm bored in the café up on the mountaintop, and my mother gives me a coin to insert in a machine that pops out a brightly painted tin egg from among the hundreds in its glass dome. The toy watch inside my egg breaks the same afternoon.

As my curly-haired aunt from Berlin is staying at Hotel

Gretel on Fremersberg, there's a party on Sunday. Senta, my German shepherd, isn't allowed to go. My aunt's borzoi is vicious and prone to bite, though he's always gentle with me.

I roam through the corridors and through the garden. In the kitchen I'm stuffed so full of cake and ice cream that I'm nearly sick to my stomach. The fat blonde kitchen maid is reproached by Dodi, the owner, a friend of my aunt's. She takes me with her to the terrace where everyone is having coffee and cake and talking in low voices about articles in the Sunday papers. Father's voice can sometimes be heard all too well. My mother then hisses his name as a warning and the subdued conversation babbles on.

I now walk to school in the morning with only Harro, who waits for me by the garage. Maria's sad face, her hand waving farewell behind the window of Father's car, appears nightly on the screen of my closed eyelids before I go to sleep. Her going away is a constant source of pain and I pray every night that she will be allowed to return.

Mia, a distantly related cousin from Frankfurt, can't take her place. While her plump face is friendly, her dark eyes are focused somewhere in the distance, not on me. She wears her brown hair in a long, thick braid, which I'm not allowed to pull. Sometimes she takes me with her for a walk on Sundays, and even carves a bird whistle out of cherry wood for me. When she meets a girlfriend who's taking care of two toddlers, she talks and talks as if I don't even exist.

The sharp jangle of the telephone on a Sunday morning

shocks Father into jumping out of bed. I've been awake for ages, and am staring at the big oval photographs of Mother's parents hanging above the red-grained headboards. Since Father's mother has moved in with us, my bed has been located across from the tall footboards of my parents' beds. This gives me ample opportunity to scrutinize the portrait of my grandfather, whom I barely knew, even though his jokes, jingling gold watch and songs in a soft foreign language still linger on vague and warm in my memory.

His face pale, Father comes back from the phone and says something in an excited whisper to Mother. The two of them get dressed rapidly, almost without saying a word. Mia is asked to take me for a walk since they have urgent business with my Aunt Mina, Grandmother's youngest sister.

It's sunny but cold, and I'm walking bare-kneed in my new Lederhosen beside Mia to the hill behind the school. She meets her girlfriend there and, walking alongside the stroller, they talk nonstop. I don't know how to play with the toddlers. Out of boredom I pluck at the grass and the flowers, whistle on blades of grass and throw stones. All of a sudden I'm assailed by a pressing need to go to the bathroom. Embarrassed to admit it so openly in front of Mia's girlfriend, I decide to go back home by myself. I begin by walking quickly and then race through streets that seem to be deserted this Sunday morning. Past Uncle Rudi's store to Leopold Square and past the movie theater in our street. Then I suddenly remember with a sinking feeling that no one is home and that my salvation lies in Aunt Mina's apartment around the corner. I pound on the door and ring the bell as if the house is on fire.

Her eyes wide with fright, Aunt Mia's daughter Irene opens the front door. When I push her aside and rush into the bathroom, she claps her hands to her buck teeth in fear.

I hear agitated voices talking all at once in the hall, and Mother wants to come in to hear what's the matter with me. She's upset and her eyes are filled with tears and for a moment I think, in a flash, that I'm to blame for it all.

Ashamed of my childish transgression, I enter the living room at her side and see my wan-faced and red-eyed relatives seated around the table. I look questioningly at my father, who says to me, almost tonelessly: "They took Uncle Adolf to Dachau last night." I don't quite understand what that means, but I know for sure that it's a thousand times worse than what's just happened to me.

The following Monday morning, my father sets off later than usual. My mother, her voice choked with emotion, says she fears for his safety, but he brushes aside her concern almost lightheartedly and says that that kind of thing can't happen to him.

I'd rather skip school today, but they both think it would be too conspicuous. Harro is waiting impatiently for me by the garage door and frowns in reproach at my tardiness. On the way to school it seems that his uncle, the blacksmith, isn't in his workshop. According to his apprentice, he didn't come home last night either.

At least ten of our classmates are standing on the school steps around Fritz in the brown uniform of the "Young

Folk." Their belt buckles are gleaming and their brown shirts have been freshly ironed, as if their club is having a party. They radiate belligerence, and the older boys, similarly outfitted in brown, treat them with more camaraderie than usual.

Fritz calls out something to me, but I either don't hear it or don't want to. Waiting in line to go inside, he hisses so loud that even Mr. Kreis can hear him: "Hey you, you little kike, are you deaf? We'll teach you a thing or two."

The boys are restless during the lesson, but Mr. Kreis does almost nothing to stop it, as if he senses that whatever is smoldering, he won't be able to put it out. During the lunch break I stick close to him, and so does Walter.

Before the gang is inside, we are the first to be sitting at our desks. Harro whispers cautiously that as soon as the last bell rings at the end of school, we should run as fast as our legs can carry us.

I don't pay any attention to the lesson and my wrong answer unleashes jeers and mean laughter from the desks in back of me. Before the bell has even stopped ringing, Harro and I leap up at the same time, not even stopping to shut our schoolbags. We run out of the classroom without saying goodbye and race down the steps with our satchels under our arms to the front door, which is just being opened. Stumbling over our own feet, gliding more than walking, we reach the street via the granite staircase. Panting, we try to catch our breath at the corner of Stephanienstrasse, where the street makes a steep climb, and see in back of us that the enemy is gathering in front of the school and that a few of them are pulling off their belts.

While running, Harro pushes his heavy pencil box to the bottom of his schoolbag, shuts it and unclasps the shoulder straps. He yells at me to do the same and to swing the bag around like a pendulum to defend myself.

I follow his example with my heart pounding and try to keep up with him. Slowly but surely, the brown and red pack catches up with us. They are strangers, our classmates. Hungry wolves in the snow.

The blacksmith's doesn't offer us any protection. The door is shut and stays shut, even after our frantic pounding. They descend on us here, with battle cries and the sound of belts whizzing through the air. Running away doesn't help. Furious, we swing our satchels like the sails of a windmill. Shaking with rage, I hit back, and feel no pain when a belt strikes me. The taunts have died down; the battle is cold and grim.

Two passers-by in work clothes order us to stop in booming voices, and suddenly it's all over. Limping and bleeding, covered with welts and scratches, we continue on home. Fritz and the rest of the herd stay where they are. We don't dare turn around.

Shaking with grief, I bury my battered, tear-stained face in my mother's chest when she opens the front door. I can't find any words.

Several days later, almost recovered, I wait for Harro at the garage door. His mother comes and says with her eyes averted that he's gone on alone. In the classroom, he's sitting in another place. Near the door, far away from me.

EMIGRATION

During Hebrew school, held in the stuffy room off the synagogue, Rabbi Grenfeld has often talked to us about the pointy Promised Land depicted on our blue collection box. Resting his left leg on the back rung of my chair or that of another child, he points the same fat index finger he uses to pick his big nose with to passages in the children's Bible and stabs angrily at letters or characters we've failed to identify correctly.

Palestine is a country from a vaguely familiar storybook tale that only starts to turn real when the bespectacled gray-haired lady comes to collect the coins in the box. She opens the flap on the bottom with a miniature key, counts the money with an expression of disappointment on her face and didactically informs us how much money is needed for that faraway land of milk and honey.

The pictures in the book she leaves behind don't bear any relation to the Bible stories I know. Farmers clearing rocky fields, plowing or picking oranges; carpenters planing boards, making furniture or building barracks; blacksmiths forging horseshoes and shoeing horses at an anvil;

mechanics tinkering with tractors; women in white head-scarves milking cows and churning butter. None of these pictures reminds me of anything in the Old Testament.

When she breathlessly relates stories of Eretz Yisrael, her eyes sparkle and red spots appear on her cheeks. My mother narrows her lips. She doesn't say a word and Father shifts impatiently in his chair. When the front door clicks behind the Zionist, he draws a deep breath in relief. Smirking, he slams the book shut, shakes his head and says that that kind of thing isn't for him. My mother hesitates and gives the book to me: Mightn't it come in handy later? For the future that no longer lies here in Germany?

School vacation is both liberation and damnation. Gray days creep by like snails. Walter and his sister Miriam have been sent on ahead to England. There's nobody to talk to or play with. A sore throat not only fails to make a dent in the solid wall of my boredom, it makes it even worse. Irritable, I lie in bed and make my mother's life miserable . . .

By trying hard, I discover I can open the train window by pulling on its broad leather strap with my full weight and then easing it open. Wind and the greasy smell of coal smoke fill the compartment. My hair flutters in the breeze and I feel the speed of the train bringing Mother and me to Freiburg. I've been allowed to come and take a look at the Children's House of the Hachschara, which trains pioneers for the country depicted on our collection box. I listen to the three-four time of the train wheels with anxious foreboding. My dread is momentarily dispelled by the sight of birds perched on the power lines like notes on a music staff, by black forests and distant blue mountains, by stations in which loud voices hawk hot sausages and eau de cologne, and by candy.

My suffocating fantasies seem to have come true when I catch sight of the big bare house with its broad stone steps and high-ceilinged rooms, in which dozens of screaming children are seated on wooden benches at long tables, eating piles of sandwiches from dented enamel plates and slurping hot skin-coated milk from tin mugs.

My mother is downstairs in the office, talking to the gray lady who sometimes comes to empty our collection box.

In a low but commanding voice, a girl who looks like Mia, except that she's fatter and has black curly hair, directs me to a place at the table. I can't swallow a bite, since my throat is constricted by despair and the fear that my mother will go away and leave me here among all these strangers and their Hebrew songs and difficult hora dances.

The children beside me shoot me scornful looks, and when my tears fall into the scum-topped milk, they show no mercy. I clamber over the bench and run to the door, where the curly-haired girl blocks my way and, friendlier than a moment ago, asks why I'm leaving the table so soon.

Determined, I push her aside, race through corridors with creaking floorboards, down stairs I don't recognize, past dormitories with beds lined up in orderly rows. I scream in mortal terror and anguish without restraint or shame and push aside anyone who tries to talk to me or hold me back. At the end of the nightmare, I see my mother standing at the bottom of the big staircase, her eyes wide with fright. She rushes to meet me. I cling to her tightly, so as never to let her go again.

In the train on the way home, I return to my senses. I'm prepared to bear anything now, anything rather than to have to go to the Promised Land alone.

I turn eight years old in Munich. We've joined my father, who is already there on business. From the window of the Metropole Hotel, I watch the bustle in the square outside the station. The streetcars, which we don't have at home, jingle and set off fireworks from their overhead lines. Every time I ask my mother why we don't take a ride on one, she avoids answering, until I understand from snatches of conversation at breakfast that public transportation is a horror for Jews. The Brownshirts can be crude and downright nasty, and she's afraid something will happen to us.

In the dining room, our breakfast table has already been set, way back in the corner. The waiter, whom Father has known for years, merely nods. He brings the honey and Father's four-minute egg after the other guests have left the room and then says softly, suddenly confidential: "I have to keep my mouth shut. I'm not allowed to know you any more." My father lowers his head and mumbles that he understands. He goes downtown to do business with a look of worry lining his face.

We meet each other again several hours later in the gloomy apartment of an aunt whom I only know from my grandmother's stories. In the meantime, Mother and I stroll through windy shopping streets and gaze at window displays in which dozens of Märklin trains race at top speed through tunnels and toy Bavarian villages, drawn by steam locomotives with real tenders. Long lines of red and green railroad cars wind their way through the mountainous landscape like gleaming snakes, and I breathlessly follow their course with my forehead pressed against the cool windowpane. Such treasures are beyond our means, but I do get a nice consolation prize for my birthday: a real Meccano set, with wheels, metal sheets, strips of nuts and bolts and smooth rods, which I carry by the wooden handle on the box.

Kneeling on one of the hard leather chairs at the glistening table in my aunt's dreary dining room, I unwrap my birthday gift. My father comes in and looks absent-mindedly at my new toy. His face is white. He says nearly inaudibly, without looking at anyone, his voice hoarse: "My oldest client has shown me the door, out of cowardice, or worse."

On the way to Moische Schwarz's, the kosher restaurant he frequented as a student, his face brightens as he regales us with anecdotes about Moische, the Polish Jew who owns the place and praises his customers in Yiddish when they eat everything on their plates. His "This one won't have to be washed" is familiar from our table at home, where Father sometimes quotes it as a joke.

Schwarz's place is very different than I'd pictured it. The three rooms of an upstairs apartment have been made into one, and the white damask-covered tables have been laid with large porcelain plates and heavy knives and forks. Linen napkins the size of aprons have been placed beside the cutlery, or else the diners, their foreheads pearled with sweat, have tied them around their necks like donkey's ears.

Huge silver-plated tureens of steaming noodle soup adorn the tables. Moische, a short fat man with a yarmulke perched on his black curls, friendly round jet-black eyes and a butcher's apron over his shirt, fishes two big meatballs from the bowl for me, because, after all, it's my birthday. At the door, he'd embraced my father like a prodigal son and commended me on my height.

He keeps coming back to take up the fourth chair at our table, and when one of the diners urgently calls him, he makes a quieting gesture with his hand and says: "Okay, okay." The diners argue heatedly with each other, turn around in their chairs to talk to whoever is behind them or to ask us questions. Whenever he can find a spare moment, Moische bombards my parents with a ceaseless flow of chatter. I try to unravel the thread of his funny German and yawn with exhaustion.

When the heavy, sweet aroma of cigar smoke has blended in with the coffee, I hear his voice, coming from way far away, saying: "You'd have to be crazy to stay in this country."

The name Effie David keeps running through my head. Mia is leaving to get married to someone in the United States. My parents talk about Effie David as if it's someone coming from the States. Might it be the daughter of my aging uncle, Grandfather's brother, the one who's a doctor in New York? Why would he be sending her to Germany?

My question of how old she is makes Mother laugh. It's not a girl, but an official document. If her elderly uncle signs it, we'll have a chance to go to safely distant North America.

Every time we pass the window of the travel agency on the way to the Spa, I admire the pictures of the ocean liners: mighty floating palaces, in which hundreds of portholes and windows are aligned in long symmetrical rows and enormous smokestacks curve towards the sky, reducing the tiny human figures on the upper decks to mere gnats as anchor cables dangle from the broad nostrils in the slender prow. HAPAG is printed in tall letters on the store's signboard, and a map of the ocean separating Europe from the U.S. shows the thin black lines along which these behemoths sail. If Grandfather's brother signs the affidavit, we might be passengers and my dream will come true.

My father opens the travel agency's big glass door as if it's something he does every day. I rejoice inwardly, but don't say anything. Mother squeezes my hand in excitement.

A man with pomaded blond hair and a natty checked suit is standing behind a tall wooden counter. Under the glass countertop are more maps crisscrossed with lines. He talks to Father about ships, money, papers and permits, and Mother listens so as not to miss a word.

I can't keep my eyes off the picture of a bearded sailor encircling the globe with his arms, the miniature freighters, but most of all, the model of an ocean liner showing every last detail, down to the swimming pool and lifeboats. It is only under silent protest that I go home with my parents, longing to know if and when we will sail.

My parents take turns knocking on Grandmother's door while calling softly or loudly "Mother" or "Mother, open the door," in urgent or beseeching tones of voice. After which they press an ear to the smooth white panel and wave a hand for silence.

I'm overcome by panic and scream through my sobs: "Grandmother, Grandmother." Senta takes fright and emits a loud, ear-splitting bark. My father roars for silence.

The lock clicks open from the inside and there is Grandmother in the doorway in a long white nightgown, with her gray hair hanging over her shoulders, her eyes glassy and her toothless gums pressed together in annoyance. Mother looks at her with a tear-stained face. Father heaps reproaches on Grandmother, who goes back to her tall wooden bedstead. Sitting on the side in her bare feet, she bursts into racking sobs. A coward, I flee to the hall, to Senta. I've never seen her like this before.

The room fills with laments and accusations. A jumble of whining voices: "I don't want to go overseas . . ." "It's all for the best . . ." "Why does it have to be so far away . . ." "You're putting us all in danger . . ." "Don't send me to *her* in Holland . . ." "Try adapting for a change . . ." "Egotist . . ." "Tyrant . . ."

The bathroom door shields me from the screams and insults. My mirror image opens its mouth and asks: "Where are we going to go?"

*

Everything about our guest is black. His name, Schwarzschild, his long hair, his eyes, the round rims of his glasses. His suit and baggy overcoat, which he even wears indoors. His shiny big shoes and floppy hat. Still, his looks don't scare me. Despite his black outlook on life, most of which is lost on me, he's kind-hearted, even friendly. A melancholy but tame crow.

He sees black clouds gathering, and is going overseas, far away. My father might be able to take his place at a factory in Chemnitz. At the dinner table, he tries to convince my father to turn down the job offer and waste no time following his example.

He spends hours reading stacks of newspapers, which grow taller every day. Only the gurgle of his black pipe and the rustle of pages being turned break the silence in the room until he jumps up to point out a passage to my parents or to read aloud an article in which Hitler and Goebbels pour their invective on the Jews.

After his departure, when the guest bed and newspapers have been cleared away, we are left behind, feeling despondent, and Father calls him Jeremiah.

The next guest is blond like Siegfried in the *Nibelungen Ring*. There's not a trace of gloom about him. He's a member of the Nazi Party, my father says, but he hasn't got anything against Jews.

My parents listen to this newly appointed manager of a factory in Mother's hometown in Saxony as they would to a stern teacher. They nod their heads eagerly when he offers to make my father a sales representative in Holland.

As his Mercedes pulls away from our apartment, they stand by the door and wave goodbye as they would to a departing friend.

I watch him from above and know where we're going.

Sunday after Sunday, we sit around the table with elderly aunts and uncles. Everywhere we encounter the same conversation, the same cinnamon stars and the same long tearful embraces and stammered words of farewell. My grandmother wants to see her brothers and sisters and the places she's known since childhood one more time. Each visit leaves my father, not normally so family-minded, wan and sad. These old people in their stuffy rooms, with their freshly waxed linoleum and spotless lace tablecloths, are also part of him. But Mother sits there looking a little out of place.

In Rastatt, one of my aging uncles has sold the last of his livestock for too little money in order to send his son Walter to the island of Cyprus. Proudly, his voice choked with tears, he displays a map in which Cyprus is pointing like a finger towards the East, towards Palestine, towards the Promised Land.

My elderly aunt is standing in the doorway when our car comes to a halt across from her house. She quickly tries to untie her apron. We're all given big kisses and I'm hugged until I can't breathe any more. Grandmother can't utter a word.

The sweet smell of pastry clings to my aging aunt. A large pot of coffee, an elegant set of china and an array of homemade cakes awaits us in the parlor. When my two male cousins and their sister Selma come in to greet us, the room is suddenly filled to capacity.

We all want to act normally, and they make polite small talk in Freistett's rustic dialect, but great gaps keep opening in the conversation. Then the only sound to be heard is the tinkling of cups and the chewing of crumbly cakes.

The strangeness gradually subsides, and my cousins dare to ask us about our departure. My aunt turns her head away to hide her tears. In the distance is the piercing hoot of the local train. The view from the tiny windows facing the village's dusty main street is suddenly obliterated by a black locomotive and two wooden boxcars which pass directly in front of the houses. The cups dance on their saucers. The conversation is drowned out by the pounding of the wheels and the deafening clang of the bell.

Selma teaches me how to play dominoes, but after a short while I prefer the company of my male cousins, who show me the goats and chickens in the farmyard.

Standing in the loft where the hay is stored, I hear my mother's frightened call for help through the heart-shaped hole in the door to the privy behind the chicken run, because a large rooster is blocking her way back to the house. My elderly aunt comes chuckling to liberate her from the confines of the outhouse, and the gloom has suddenly been lifted.

Kneeling on the back seat of Father's dark-blue Adler, I watch my relatives grow smaller and smaller, until they are finally obscured by a billowing cloud of dust.

*

While the drive to the iron bridge over the Rhine at Kehl is short, our fear is long. The guards are standing at the approach to the bridge in their green uniforms, steel helmets or stiff green caps.

My grandmother, gasping for air in all the turmoil, is given a spoonful of pungent valerian drops by my mother.

Someone snarls an order for us to get out. Grandmother is allowed to stay in the car. One of the officials empties the jars and bottles in the leather beauty case onto a long, metal-edged wooden table and screws off all the lids. He pokes through my father's papers and orders my parents to step inside the customs shed to be searched. I wait by the suitcase and stammer with fright when a steel helmet asks me what I have with me.

They return, silently, their faces pale. As we pass through the barrier, it's deathly still. I only hear them breathe again when we reach the other side, where the French customs officials are standing, as if they've been holding their breath the entire time. My grandmother opens her eyes and pats my hand.

The mustached guards in dark-blue uniforms with red piping give the passports a cursory glance. One of them inundates us with a rapid flow of French until my mother understands that he wants to check the trunk. But when he catches sight of my grandmother in the back seat, he waves his hand with a slight laugh in a gesture of "never mind" and motions us to continue on our way.

Near the guardhouse, an old man is waving his umbrella back and forth like a windshield wiper. He greets us with a grin and removes his black Homburg with a flourish towards his sister. Uncle Edward kisses us on both cheeks with his damp, cigar-stained mustache and holds Grandmother even longer than he does us. She drives into Strasbourg seated beside him in the lead car. Timbered houses, cathedrals, broad squares and flowering embankments race past as in a dream. The cars come to a stop by a restaurant called "The Crocodile." A Frenchman in a dark beret, who turns out to be a cousin speaking a language I can't understand, is waiting for us to arrive.

We file through spacious, dimly lit, thickly carpeted rooms, past elegantly attired diners who are conversing softly or eating their meals in silence, poised like worshippers before their plates and wineglasses. A green-glazed crocodile is squirting gurgling water into a fountain. The maître d' makes a deep bow to my white-haired uncle and leads us to a screened-off corner of a room illuminated by green and white Tiffany glass. The rows of cutlery and stemware at every plate except mine presage a long, boring sit.

After the waiter has filled the outermost glasses, Uncle Edward solemnly raises his goblet and talks with tears in his eyes about freedom and family reunions, about his sisters and brothers and about Verdun and "les Boches," who could learn a thing or two from France.

Cousin Rolf is a man of few words. It is only after the interminable lunch, when my eyes are burning from cigar smoke and sleep, that I hear my father from far away ask him to take some valuables to Holland for us.

Shortly after these words, late in the afternoon, we return to the country that hates us.

Senta is dead, Senta is dead, Senta is dead. I sob these words into my pillow to the beat of my heart. I'm disconsolate, even though my parents had promised me a new dog for the new country. Senta was sick, Senta was sick, Senta was . . .

She had looked at me this morning with her big kind German shepherd eyes, her ears cocked vigilantly, her tail swishing back and forth like a metronome.

"She can't go with us," "She's sick," "She isn't allowed into the country . . ." I didn't want to hear a word of it this morning, not another word.

I bury my sorrow in her black fur.

Wagging her tail, she goes with Father, sick but happy.

He comes back with his hands empty. Not even her collar!

I steal her oval portrait from the photo album and tuck it away as my most treasured possession.

Three hulking men clump over the floorboards of our apartment. The carpets have already been rolled up. Tables and chairs are stacked atop each other or lined up against the walls. The men don grimy brown aprons, roll up their shirtsleeves and in rapid tempo start packing chinaware, books and any object that comes their way in newspaper. Gently but firmly, they deposit each item in the wooden packing crates with their huge, dusty, ink-stained hands. They shout back and forth in incomprehensible Dutch in the hollow rooms, crack jokes and then burst into peals of laughter. Filled with curiosity, I watch their rapid fingers and their muscular, veined arms. The blue tattoos of women and hearts both fascinate and repel me.

My mother wants to help, but the items she trots out are snatched from her hands only to disappear among the rest of the household goods, wrapped beyond recognition in newspaper.

She warns me not to get in the way or to keep the men from their work, but one of them says good-naturedly in the same funny German as my Dutch aunt that I'm not a bother.

My father stomps irritably through the apartment, issuing instructions which are seldom obeyed by the movers because they either don't understand what he says or don't want to.

He takes it out on Mother and me, but never so loud that the men can hear it. He is anxiously solicitous about scratches and marks on the furniture, especially his darling, the grand piano. The movers, pearls of sweat beading their red faces, lug the heavy piano through the hallways and down the stairs. They pant and groan and hiss advice, the straps around their necks and shoulders taut as a tightrope, until they reach the moving van on the sidewalk. My parents remain upstairs, pale and resigned.

Downstairs, a German in a green Alpine hat with a feather has been standing by the burlap-lined loading doors for hours, with a black leather briefcase at his feet and a piece of chalk in his hand. He assigns a number to every item loaded in the truck and writes it down in his book. He doesn't say a word to either my parents or the movers, and he merely frowns at their jokes. He suspiciously checks the bolting of the doors and seals the locks with lead.

The apartment is hollow and empty. The white front door, behind which Senta had guarded the house, falls shut behind us. The click echoes sharply in the stairwell. No one hears it and no one comes to wave us goodbye.

My house is gone, my room is gone, my dog is gone, my toys are gone, everything is gone, gone, gone. No more Harro, no more school. Even my teddy bear is gone. All that I have left is what's in the suitcase on the back seat of the car, in what should have been Grandmother's place. But she has been sent on ahead to Rotterdam by train. I watched her disappear from view, seated in the compartment as if she were being led to slaughter, moaning that she wouldn't survive the journey.

Cities and villages glide past, milestone after milestone. When hunger, thirst or some other inconvenience obliges my father to stop, we start looking for an inn, a hotel or a café without a "No Jews Allowed" sign on the door. Often, we have to resume our journey without having found a safe place to stop. So we keep driving until we find a patch of grass or a bench where we can eat the food we've purchased along the way. It's like a picnic, but without the fun.

Father's Adler hums along past forests and over hills, monotonously devouring the ribbon of asphalt or brick until darkness falls.

We're exhausted, absolutely exhausted, by the time the signs for München Gladbach come into view. We go from hotel to hotel to hotel and are shown the door as if we were a bunch of bums. At the end of the line is a pension: owned by Jews, for Jews.

Sleep eludes me, and I have no more tears left.

Curtains are blowing gently in the breeze. Through the windows, I watch the stars shine down on my last night in the country of my birth.

"WE DIDN'T KNOW ANYTHING"

Epilogue

Offenburg, Appenweier, Achern: names on signposts along backroads, vague echoes from my childhood.

We drive into the lowland plains of the Rhineland from the misty, rainy, blue-green woods of the Black Forest. Heading back to Holland from Switzerland, we take the route passing through the country of my birth.

At the border, I feel a fifty-year-old rudiment of the fear that I will be denied permission to cross and a tingle of triumph when the official gestures us through without even checking our passports.

The Dutch license plates on my small red Citroën, my wife at my side and my youngest daughter asleep on the back seat of the car inspire the trust of border guards at every frontier. I'm no longer an undesirable refugee, but a tourist with a wallet full of hard currency.

Freistett, an almost imperceptible dot on the map, is located near the Rhine, in the flatlands which various rulers have been contesting and subsequently neglecting for centuries.

Can I interrupt our homeward journey after a sunny vacation on Lake Leman to conjure up fifty-year-old ghosts? The name Freistett casts a spell on me, attracts me, attracts the child in me who from the back seat of the blue Adler watched his relatives disappear from his life in a cloud of dust.

I guide the car through the Dutch-like landscape, along straight and quiet roads, past small villages. Without a word, I drive as my father drove. I see what he saw, what I saw. For a moment, I am him.

I miss the turnoff at the junction. Do I really want to see and hear? After a right turn, I see the retouched photo of my memory, two hundred yards ahead of us. Sand and dust have made way for asphalt. The train track has disappeared. Sidewalks, new and clean, line both sides of the street. The houses are painted pink, green and yellow; the stores have modern fronts: a perfect Potemkin village.

Yet everything is also the same: the front doors on the left, the barn doors on the right, the overhanging eaves, the flat red and black roof tiles.

I look for my aunt's house. It looks familiar and yet unfamiliar at the same time, now a store selling stationery, cigars and newspapers. The urban-born saleslady doesn't know anything about who owned it or who lived in it long ago. The owner appears, but my memory is older than he is; he directs me to his somewhat older neighbor, who owns the liquor store on the right. We find her elderly mother-in-law, whose gray hair is pulled back into a tight bun the way village women wore their hair in my youth, behind the store. Her son, whose hair is nearly gray, does the talking. A grin is plastered to his broad face, which changes from suspicious to shy, back to guarded and then to open, serious.

Did he used to know my aunt and my cousins?

Why, they were friends and good neighbors!

He leads us to the farmyard behind his house. A black and tan German shepherd bares his teeth and jumps furiously against the bars of his cage as if he feels his owner's apprehension. He calls to an elderly neighbor hanging up her wash in my Aunt Hermine's barnyard, the back of the house with the stationery store.

Nothing is changed, nothing has been remodeled. The barn door, the hayloft, the ditch housing the privy . . . a remembrance that evokes a laugh, as it was torn down ten years ago.

The conversation continues in broad dialect over our heads. About you but without you. "Remember Bertha next door and half-witted Rosel?"

The old women and the son untangle the branches of my family tree, including those I didn't know I had.

A bashful silence falls when I answer their question of what became of *us*. The names of camps fall like stones into a ravine. The neighbor watches me nervously, his eyes restless, his fingers picking at a button: "We didn't know anything, 'they' didn't tell us anything during the war."

Then suddenly confidential, giggling, he confides half to us and half to the women around us that during his youth, fathers used to threaten their sons with a new punishment: concentration camp. Kuhberg concentration camp wasn't too far away, and the rumors had trickled into their daily life. Still, he assured us, no one in the village knew anything then about the "Final Solution to the Jewish Question." They only heard about that after the war, and couldn't understand what had happened to "all those Jews".

Self-assured, his moral whitewash continues. He watches me from the corner of his eye while scoffing at the Allies, the French and the Dutch, who according to him knew everything and still played Judas. Irrepressible, he proceeds further: his father had served in Dachau, in the black uniform of the SS, but his conscience had buckled under the strain. Even before the war, he came home shattered, and refused to carry out the brutish deeds any longer.

What should I say in my doubt, my uncertainty? What did they know, what had they had to banish from their minds in order to live?

I want to get away, away from the place where my ailing aunt watched her dilapidated store and house being ravaged before her eighty-year-old eyes on Kristallnacht in November 1938. My head is pounding with anger as we head back to the street past the furiously barking dog.

But angry at whom?

At old Gustave, his leg injured on the Eastern Front, who limps his way towards us to dredge up his reminiscences of my dead relatives? At Hilda, the farm laborer with a hoe on her shoulder and baskets of vegetables hanging from the rusty handlebars of her bicycle, who tells us in a minimum of words that she had once worked for my family?

Angry at the evil fate that had struck European Jewry?

My daughter is sitting on the back seat of the car with her Walkman on her ears. We drive off. The old people wave.

We wave back, our hearts filled with doubt and confusion.

We're home by nightfall, faster than the first time. And free.

This time I'm driving through a green no man's land, with my gaze fixed on infinity, my foot pressed firmly on the gas pedal: the German autobahn.

No chance to dwell on thoughts of the past. While Hitler's strategically planned superhighways provide an efficient way to travel from south to north, it's dangerous to daydream.

Cities are reduced to nothing more than names on blue freeway signs, words in an atlas. Until suddenly a double-barreled name demanding catharsis looms up at me: Baden-Baden; my birthplace and childhood home.

This time it's curiosity that draws me to the place. Years ago, I had once paid heed to the wishes of my wife and children to turn off in the direction of my youth. I viewed the town that time as if I were a stranger, and cordoned off any emotions that might be painful. Later, in the safety and protection of my analyst's couch, the images arose along with my tears of grief and rage, and I was able to accept my boyhood years for what they were.

Only a few more miles to go: we're driving past the old blocks of yellow apartment buildings on the outskirts of town. It doesn't seem very familiar. My childhood radius didn't extend this far. All of a sudden, as we near the center of town, everything comes back to me. Then and now come together. The rose bushes, the flower beds, the crystal-clear bubbling Murg, the five-star hotels, which make even the row of Mercedes Benzs parked out front pale in comparison, the Pump Room with its formerly scary and now merely repulsive murals of knights, dragons and pale virgins, the sidewalk cafés with their gaily colored umbrellas and white painted chairs: everything is the same and yet different. Now there are girls in shorts and boys in jeans. Then there were men in panama hats and women in silk dresses.

Grandmother's furniture store, unchanged, still owned by the man whose name was uttered in anger at home. And Bismarck still stares implacably into the distance.

We proceed on foot, ordinary sightseers exploring the town. I look at buildings not likely to interest tourists and know exactly where my feet are taking me. I stop in front of my school. I've never been away, nothing has changed. Harro and I fled down these steps to Stephanienstrasse. Now the incline makes me feel my years. Breathing hard, I stand on the spot where we turned our schoolbags into weapons and hunt for signs of the place where the synagogue once stood. My wife and daughter follow me as they would a sleepwalker, concerned for my safety.

The white stone synagogue, with its slender pillars, arched windows, multi-colored rosettes and broad staircase whose steps I had trouble climbing as a child, no longer exists. It has been replaced by a garage housing a few trucks. Not a trace remains of the place where, on the evening of 9 November 1938, black-uniformed SS men forced elderly Jews to uncover their heads and sing Nazi songs, with their faces turned towards the Ark containing the holy Torah scrolls, which flicker like the burning bush after having been set ablaze under the roars and jeers of the Death Head Regiment.

The snapshots which one of the SS men took as an amusing souvenir and which had been tucked away for decades in archives have been indelibly etched in my mind. The burning house of prayer, shrouded in soot and smoke, the hatless old men, forced to march in columns, with their pale uncomprehending faces sticking out above their dark overcoats, exhausted by recruit drills and mortal terror: Kristallnacht.

"We didn't know anything, well hardly anything" is still the answer anticipating the question and reducing it to silence.

In this curve in Stephanienstrasse, it torments me.

This is not a country of the blind, the deaf and the dumb. Anyone who wanted to hear could hear. Anyone who wanted to see could see. The speeches in which hoarse demagogues proclaimed our destruction were blared from every loudspeaker since January 1933. The measures aimed at isolating us, which daily chipped away at our freedom, were printed in big bold letters in every newspaper.

Countless Germans allowed themselves to be led into barbarism.

Countless Germans, indifferent or paralyzed by fear, watched us drowning before their eyes.

And a few of them, courageous like Fritz the waiter in Riva on Lake Garda, rescued one of the drowning from the waves.

Also published by Serpent's Tail

Stripes in the Sky
Gerhard Durlacher

The prisoners in the concentration camp Auschwitz-Birkenau saw stripes in the sky in August 1944, as allied bombers flew over their camp. After having destroyed a nearby industrial target, the bombers returned home, leaving the prisoners to wonder why the camp's gas chambers and crematoria had not been bombed and the factory of death destroyed.

"Moving and angry." *The Sunday Times*

"Powerful and moving account by one of the survivors of Auschwitz. His graphic description of bombs dropping near his Dutch home, of progression through the camps and ultimately of liberation and return to his home is fresh, without self-pity and utterly real." *Scotland on Sunday*